Trust Issues:

The Complete Guide to Overcoming Trust Issues One Step at a Time

Author: **Herman Kynaston**

© Copyright 2019 - All rights reserved.

The content contained within this book may not be reproduced, duplicated or transmitted without direct written permission from the author or the publisher.

Under no circumstances will any blame or legal responsibility be held against the publisher, or author, for any damages, reparation, or monetary loss due to the information contained within this book. Either directly or indirectly.

Legal Notice:

This book is copyright protected. This book is only for personal use. You cannot amend, distribute, sell, use, quote or paraphrase any part, or the content within this book, without the consent of the author or publisher.

Disclaimer Notice:

Please note the information contained within this document is for educational and entertainment purposes only. All effort has been executed to present accurate, up to date, and reliable, complete information. No warranties of any kind are declared or implied. Readers acknowledge that the author is not engaging in the rendering of legal, financial, medical or professional advice. The content within this book has been derived from various sources. Please consult a licensed professional before attempting any techniques outlined in this book.

By reading this document, the reader agrees that under no circumstances is the author responsible for any losses, direct or indirect, which are incurred as a result of the use of information contained within this document, including, but not limited to, — errors, omissions, or inaccuracies.

Table of Contents

Book Description: 1
Introduction 3
Chapter One What Are Trust Issues? 4
    Signs You May Have Trust Issues 4
    Signs Someone You Know or Don't Know has Trust Issues 7
Chapter Two What Causes Trust Issues? 12
    How Childhood Events can Cause Difficulties with Trust 12
    Where do Trust Issues Come From? 15
    The Neuroscience behind Trust 16
    How Exactly Does This Work? 17
    What is Pistanthrophobia? 18
Chapter Three Trust Issues in Relationships 21
    What is Trust? 22
    Reasons we May Find it hard to Trust the Ones we Love 24
    Trust Issues within a Friendship 28
    Reasons you are Unable to Trust Your Boss 32
    Signs that Trust Issues are Affecting Your Marriage 36
    Learning How to Trust Your New Spouse 40
Chapter Four Dealing With Trust Issues 47
    Signs You Don't Trust Yourself 47
    How to Take Hold of Your Trust Issues 49
Chapter Five Fixing the Problem 54
    Overcoming Trust Issues in a Partnership 54
    How to Overcome Trust Issues 59
    Dealing With Self-Doubt. Trust Yourself 61

Overcome Fear to Trust Yourself Again.. 63

Chapter Six Building Trust 66
How to Build Trust in Yourself.. 66
Ways to Rebuild Trust in Your Relationships.. 70

Conclusion..77

Bonus Material: Earning – An Introduction To Earning With The Double Your Income Sequence..78
Section 1: The Secret Of Forming Money Habits (And How To Enforce Them).. 78
Section 2: How To Create New Money Habits 79
Section 3: The 14 Habits That Will Double Your Income 81
Section 4: The Golden Rule Of Success Sequencing.................................... 96
Section 5: These Habits Will Matter Most! 97
Section 6: Willpower Or Wontpower: You Decide.. 98
Section 7: Regaining Your Faith In Free Will 99

Check Out Our Other Books: 101
1. *Resolving Anxiety and Panic Attacks* 101
2. *Cognitive Behavioral Therapy* 103
3. *Effective Guide On How to Sleep Well Everyday*................................... 105
Dangers of Sleep deprivation. 106
How Much Sleep Do I Really Need? 108
Understand what Kind of a Sleeper Are You? 110
Simple techniques of preparing for bed.. 115
A Few Lifestyle Suggestions to Make You Sleep Better 117

References..119

Book Description

Do you find yourself suspicious, mistrustful and regularly doubting others motives? Trust issues can rob you of intimacy, real friendships and closeness with those around you.

People may have hurt you in the past, but if this is negatively impacting your present – you're keeping yourself from finding personal happiness. You don't have to live this way. Feelings of jealousy, suspicion, betrayal, and loneliness all come from the same root cause – fear!

In *Overcoming Trust Issues,* I deconstruct why your emotional default has become mistrust. Then, I take you through a rigorous process of step-by-step healing, so that you can open yourself up to others again, without fear. Recover from your trust issues, by understanding yourself.

In this useful guide you'll learn:

- The signs that you have serious trust issues to overcome
- The traumatic causes of developing trust issues
- How trust issues manifest with partners, friends and family
- What you can do to start healing from these destructive patterns
- How to actively build real trust in your life
- How to overcome the trust issues that have kept you from happiness

This complete guide will reframe how you see trust and use it in your life. Your old ways are not working. A better path lies ahead, and it begins with positive change.

Take the leap and face the trust issues you've been running from since childhood. It's not too late! Find real closeness and genuine relationships when you realize it's you that needs to heal!

Discover the healing power of trust in this guide.

Buy it now and love again!

Introduction

In this book, I will walk you through the importance of trust, and what trust issues are. You will learn how to come to terms with your experiences surrounding trust issues, and understand where it comes from. After learning the details about trust issues, you will be able to understand more about how to fix the problem and understand the steps to take to self-love and awareness. No matter what age you are, what gender, what life stage you are at and what type of relationship you have, it is time to gain insight on all of the ways to live healthier. By the end of this eBook, you will have a better understanding of what makes you have this problem, how to fix it and be set up for being on the road to living a better life for yourself and the people around you.

Chapter One
What Are Trust Issues?

"To be trusted is a greater compliment than being loved." – George MacDonald

Trust issues are when a person has an extremely difficult time trusting others due to any personal or non-personal reasons. Trust issues can be due to actions or the lack thereof of the other person, which can be anyone, such as a spouse or partner, a friend, family members and/or complete strangers. Trust issues are a great problem to have because it will cause issues in future events like missing out on meaningful situations in life.

Signs You May Have Trust Issues

Trust issues can come in different forms, and in different ages, or stages of one person's lifetime. A woman or a man may be showing signs of distrust if one constantly asks where the other has been, and even though one spouse may be telling the truth, the other will convince themselves otherwise.

A young boy or girl meets his parent's new spouse for the first time. He or she wants to be polite and respectful, but cannot contain the thoughts that spin in their mind that this new partner will leave and never return; this stems from past abandonment.

A person with a diagnosed health problem is unwilling to accept he or she doesn't have a problem, and so demands constant second opinions that all lead to the same results. This stems from a genetic problem that kept going unnoticed until it was too late from a past relative.

Many of us have feelings of betrayal, abandonment, and manipulation. These feelings are fears that would describe why someone would develop a trust issue of some sort. As I have said, trust issues can come in many forms; one situation being a partner cheats or is disloyal, and so there is an irrational fear that he or she could do it again - feelings of paranoia. Another situation is that a child's mother or father has left or abandoned them at too young an age, so anyone who will come into their lives could potentially leave - feelings of betrayal. A different circumstance being afraid that doctors or health practitioners are not taken seriously due to a misleading diagnosis from a relative that passed away with the unnoticed prognosis.

Have you had similar instances in your life equally, more or less traumatic? Are you unsure if it has led to some sort of distrust with yourself or even others? Let's figure it out with this list of signs that you could potentially be at risk for having trust issues:

- **You presume betrayal**

Even though you have no proof or reason to judge, you automatically or instinctively assume someone has betrayed you.

- **You expect betrayal**

No matter how honest or loyal someone has been up until now, you constantly suspect they will betray you. They have given you no reason, but you suspect there will come a day where they will prove you right. You act like this for an extended amount of time.

- **You are extremely protective**

You are fearful that your loved ones will become disloyal or dishonest, so you become overly protective. You are protective of them by questioning them constantly about your irrational fears. You are also protective of yourself, being careful not to let your walls down.

- **You become distant from others**

Because of unreasonable fears due to traumatic experiences, you avoid or limit contact with relationships in your life. You are also afraid to get close to anyone for fears in relation to them betraying or leaving you.

- **You avert from commitment**

You are afraid of commitment, so you avoid it at all costs. You protect your heart and so you do your best to avoid attachment no matter how much you care for, or love someone. This includes a spouse, health practitioner, friends, acquaintances, employees, and family members, etc.

- **It is hard to forgive**

Even for the smallest mistakes from someone else, it takes you a long time to forget. You tend to make a big deal out of small stuff or create arguments to push people away when they get too close.

- **You are cautious of people unnecessarily**

Every time you meet someone new, you are quick to put up walls. You watch their every move and get to know them before they get to know you.

- **You often feel lonely or depressed**

Because of your fears or traumatic experiences, you find it hard to open up and find yourself alone. Due to you isolating yourself, you become depressed. You are entering, or have entered the state of depression, alongside being lonely.

Signs Someone You Know or Don't Know has Trust Issues

Aside from yourself having these signs, you may notice these signs in others as well. It is harder to tell if someone else has trust issues until you get to know them better but, if you notice any signs of distrust traits, make sure to give them plenty of space and be patient. People with trust issues do not give trust easily, and will not return it as fast as you might. Trust issues in people are not to be taken lightly and it is not up to you to judge them either. If you give them lots of time and space to open up to you, then their real personality will shine brighter than the issue they have. Be careful with these types of people because once the trust is broken, it is extremely difficult to get it back and may cause problems for your relationship. Here is how to tell if someone else has trust difficulties. Not all of these signs are present:

- **They are reserved and less emotional**

    People who generally have trust problems will show signs of withdrawal. They do not want to feel vulnerable, so they use less emotion because it is easier for them to shell up rather than expose themselves. This results from a fear of becoming attached to anyone due to abandonment or difficult past experiences. These people come off as cold, unfriendly, and often anti-social.

- **They are perpetually skeptical**

    For people who have major distrust, they are generally cautious of others. For them, their fears are magnified as if they had an anxiety disorder; constantly on edge or worried but not of themselves, only of others. If this person is questioning and concerned at an abnormal level, any unexplained event or situation that doesn't add up is a threat. Their uncertainty will distract them from the truth and make them believe what they want to believe, forcing them to think irrationally.

- **They avert from human communication**

It is not uncommon for someone to isolate themselves if they have an irrational fear of trust from others. They become anti-social, thus leaving them lonely, and disengaged. In this case, the person may believe they are protecting themselves from being hurt, and becoming involved with a 'bad' person.

- **They seem discourteous**

By coming off as unfriendly or unwelcoming, is a self-coping mechanism to help protect themselves from 'unsafe' people or environments. These people will be hard to get to know and may push you away. This is not necessarily their intention, but they believe that they are testing who comes into their lives to stay long enough to be able to trust.

- **They seem 'bipolar' or sensitive to triggers**

Say you are talking to someone, and out of nowhere they become instantly sad and defensive without you accusing them of anything. The intention you had was not to make them feel attacked, and then a fight or argument breaks out because you may have accidentally triggered them. This is not to say they are 'bipolar,' but it will happen when someone has severe trust issues or difficulty with trust. In many cases, these triggers are imaginative and not real. It is, however, very real for them.

- **They take what you say wrong more times than not**

Do you have to rephrase your communication? Does someone ask you what you mean and ask you to explain yourself often? Having trust issues is based on having psychological wounds. People with distrust will respond with statements like these because you may have triggered them, or what you are saying is not making sense to them because they have a different defined meaning behind your every word. Difficulties with trust can result in having a faulty perspective in the world around them.

- **They come off as judgmental and may hate for no apparent reason**

Without you doing anything wrong or even having the intentions of wronging someone, they may judge you, have negative thoughts and feelings about you or even hate you. These are based upon wrong calculations inside their own head.

- **They also fear commitment and attachment**

People who have a difficult time with trust may fear intimacy because they are afraid of becoming hurt. They fear to open themselves up due to the lack of trust they have for others and seem vulnerable and weak. It is nothing to do with you, but in their own mind, they cannot connect with you on the same level as their trust dial is turned up way too high.

- **They won't assign tasks**

People with this trait have a hard time letting go of control which can result in delegating tasks to others because of trust - or lack thereof.

- **They are, or become introverts**

An introvert is someone who would rather be by themselves, in their own world than hang out with others. People are introverts for many reasons, whether it be a personality trait or, in more serious cases, a personality disorder. Someone that struggles with trust becomes introverted because they feel it is to protect themselves from others and the world around them due to many complications.

This list is not to say people with all these signs and/or symptoms is a person who has trust issues. This list was designed to find who requires help and for information for yourself. A person with trust issues will NOT act like this all the time, but only when their trust has been broken, or they are meeting you for the first time. I always say it is best to get to know someone before defining who they are. Find their good traits and their bad, and either live with it or walk away from it. A person who struggles with trust can be the best person in the world to hang out with once you get to know them. The only thing they have a hard time with is giving out trust as easily as they are getting it. They don't care whether they get your trust, just as long as your trust is never broken. This sometimes leads to no room for mistakes which is irrational thinking because it is only human nature to make mistakes.

The two lists are given and laid out like this because it is to tell the difference between when you have trust issues, and how to tell if someone else has trust issues. If you read this properly, you will be able to see two different perspectives based on your own, and how others feel as well.

If you find out you or someone you know has trust issues, the best thing to do is try not to be judgmental. Everyone has a past, and everyone has different experiences. Difficulties with trusting someone or multiple people have underlying causes that only they can find out for themselves and vice versa - you can find out for yourself. The strength in all this is to find out how to come out on top, and how to get better. When you acknowledge that there is a problem, you can seek help and make changes to fix it if you want to lead a healthy life.

Chapter Two
What Causes Trust Issues?

"Trust starts with truth and ends with truth" – Santosh Kalwar

Many things cause trust issues. We can go as far back as childhood experiences that were traumatic to the individual, such as abandonment and neglect. It can be based on science and how an individual's brain processes on how trust works. It can be caused by feelings of being betrayed by a significant other, or someone fairly close to us. Difficulties with trust also have fear attached to it which is called Pistanthrophobia.

Studies show, as proven by psychologists, that, in the last ten years, there has been an incredible rise in trust issues among relationships who seek couples counseling. As Joe Bayonese, Relationship Institute says, the main reason for the rise on trust issues is due to technological advancement. Technology makes it easier for couples to hide text messages, cell phone calls lists, social media friends' messages and emails. This is called being deceptive.

Trust is one of the top things people care about in the world, as it is one of the easiest things to get broken, and one of the hardest things to gain back.

How Childhood Events can Cause Difficulties with Trust

People don't realize that the younger you are, the more crucial it is to have a basic routine and great structure from your parents. If a child doesn't get what he or she needs, or the traumatizing experience is too harsh, it can set their future as adults up for problems, such as having difficulties with trust.

Many circumstances involved with childhood past relate to why we have a hard time trusting people in our lives now. As we grow and develop into who we are going to be, we develop a personality which comes with preferences, morals, perspectives, values, and views. This personality concludes what we think about ourselves, others and affect how we respond to situations that we are faced with. Some key factors play a part with distrust, which is caused by, or related to, childhood trauma:

- Emotional and verbal abuse
- Sexual and physical abuse
- Mental and other abuse
- Neglect and abandonment

A child does not necessarily have to go through the abuse; it may just be enough to see it happening to someone they love. Some other things that stem from early trust issue problems for their future are:

- A traumatic injury
- Illness
- Surgery
- A family crisis
- Divorce
- Death of a parent or loved one
- An unstable/busy household

- Inconsistencies in parenting

This is not a complete list but, as the child grows older, all these take a huge effect on how they will perceive trust, and who they CAN trust. The development of trust issues begins early and can be difficult to handle if you don't know the signs. Let's not forget to mention the fact that what causes the issue can be from feelings of betrayal, and self-worth.

As humans, we are emotional beings and what we feel, and how we feel, will affect the way and how we live our lives. If we were neglected or abandoned at any given time in our lives, we would most likely be careful not to be so quick to trust the next person who says they will stick around. A good quote I once heard was "People will come into your life for a reason, a season or a lifetime." As social beings, we look for people who will stick around for a lifetime.

If we have been abused in any way throughout any stage in our lives, mostly as kids, we will be more susceptible to what we allow in our future. This means that a person with trust issues may look bad to the outsider but, to the individual, it is believable enough that they are only trying to protect themselves against the 'bad' influences.

A child who grew up in a family with siblings may lash out with distrusting others as they might feel that is the best coping mechanism for them, to be able to stand on their own. Everyone wants to be independent and self-worthy so, if our childhoods were hectic, we are only going to want to do the opposite of that in our futures - thus trust issues.

Because children are constantly looking for their peers for guidance, what they see will largely impact what they become. Example: If a child was to see their parents upset all the time, mad or just plain flawed, they will unintentionally blame themselves. If this happens, they come out of their childhood feeling bad about themselves (not trusting themselves) and feeling insecure about life and how others portray them; hence, not trusting others now as well.

Now that I have covered only the borderline of what causes trust issues when you are a child, there is a different topic that concludes other causes of being a distrustful person. Some people may never experience a traumatic childhood, and therefore just need constant reassurance because they are insecure. This may or may not cause problems in a relationship (we will get to this later), so, what else is there?

Where do Trust Issues Come From?

Aside from childhood trauma, or just plain past trauma, where else do trust issues stem from? Trust usually takes years to develop and seconds to destroy, but what is it about trust that has people so unwilling to give it away? People with trust issues have, in most cases, trusted someone or an organization of some sort that has let them down. Once this happens, we usually try not to make the same mistakes again. Think of it as a chain – you are the most trusting person in the world, you give everyone the benefit of the doubt until that someone breaks your trust by doing something negative towards or against you. You think to yourself 'not going to make that mistake again,' so the next time you are presented with a similar situation you are a little more careful, and they end up breaking your trust. Sometimes, all it comes down to is people breaking your trust so much that you just stop giving it away.

What sucks about that is the people who actually can be trusted don't get trusted because of, again, personal and past experiences.

Negative outcomes develop trust issues to a situation or from another individual. A negative childhood can lead to distrust from your peers; social rejection in school-aged students can lead to distrust of friends and unsupportive family members, and traumatic experiences in adulthood can lead to trust issues for a certain type of individual.

Trust issues stem from feelings of betrayal, and insecurities within oneself. A romantic relationship that was unfaithful or dishonest can set an adult up to have trust issues for life. Distrust towards institutions stems from contracts being broken, or a company shutting down.

Once someone's trust is broken many times in many ways, the person is bound to be affected, causing future difficulties putting trust in others or organizations.

The Neuroscience behind Trust

A recent study has shown that our brains thrive on instinct to trust others. Due to being social creatures, we instinctively want to let people in and have the close trusting bond that we need for comfort. By having our trust broken, it short circuits our neurobiology making it difficult to trust again.

Imagine you are in a position where you made great friends with someone. You put your trust in them, you grow a bond with them, and you start to tell them your secrets and BAM, they betray your trust.

When this happens, the neural networks in our brains disengage and shut down, making sure to remember this event and what was associated with it. The once- positive emotions towards this person had been replaced with animosity, suspicion, resentment, and maybe some confusion. Our brains are the smartest computers of all time. It is continuously making connections and disconnecting patterns and so on. When your brain compartmentalizes the betrayal and files all the positive and sets aside the negative of this person, it files it at such a fast pace that, once you snap back to reality, your brain was only waiting for you to catch up, and is waiting for you to make a decision based on this betrayal.

How Exactly Does This Work?

There was a recent test done on students. The participants were to be under the illusion that they were playing an investment game with three different players - someone they knew to be close to them, someone they didn't know, and a computerized slot machine. What the participants did not know was that they were playing against a computer with simple algorithms that methodically reciprocated actions based on, or related to trust exactly 50% of the time.

These were the results: The participants who thought they were playing against a close relation reported positive interactions, and had more rewarding results than that of a stranger or slot machine. This way, they invested more with their close relations partner, and not so much with the other two players. This states that our unconditioned human nature desires to connect with others and create close bonds, regarding of the fact if it is someone we don't know as this can lead to silly schemes.

When the participants thought they were playing with a close relation, brain imaging showed that the ventral striatum and medial prefrontal cortex were more actively engaged compared to when they thought they were playing with a computer or stranger. These two brain regions were correlated with positive social value signals when the participants made choices based solely on the belief they were playing with a close relation.

The medial prefrontal cortex is the part of the brain that is associated with how we perceive someone else's mental state and monitoring what happens outside the focus of our current attention. It is also associated with decision-making and retrieving and combining memories.

During the game, these two brain regions provide evidence that when we talk to close friends or family, people we trust, we feel a greater social reward, and co-operate better, than if we talk to or invest time into a stranger or computerized machine. Regardless, the participants who played the game still wanted to trust the computer and stranger. This shows that as we are social creatures, our instincts are to trust or to want to trust whomever.

The results of this study suggest the willingness to trust others is part of our DNA. With this being said, people that do have trust issues are in the hope that they can, and will find relief, and be able to live a healthier life. It will take work and structure in order for this to happen, but it is possible.

On the other hand of this test, the experiment also suggests that the instinct to trust can override logic. People can be easily tricked when the 'supposed close relation' is no more than a computerized machine. When betrayal takes a part of us and the feelings associated with it, the reason it is so traumatic is the underlying vulnerability of blind trust this test illustrates. We want to trust people due to our neurobiological roots, but only genuine trust has to be earned.

In conclusion: It is a good thing to have trust issues in some cases, but not all. In a world full of scammers, having a healthy dose of skepticism is a good idea.

What is Pistanthrophobia?

Pistanthrophobia is the fear of having or building an intimate and personal relationship with other people. Because of past trauma, the fear of trusting others becomes stronger than the need to be close and intimate.

People with Pistanthrophobia feel as if everyone they become close to will disappoint, or betray them in some way - one way or another. Their fear takes over to the point that they will believe it is better to be alone than to let the past repeat itself.

Behaviors of Pistanthrophobia are a lot like trust issue behaviors. The signs and symptoms are very similar. They become anti-social and isolate themselves, much like someone with trust issues would do. Here are some signs that you may have Pistanthrophobia:

- Averting from any activities involving close interpersonal contact.
- Due to the fear of criticism, they become withdrawn.
- They have an extreme fear of being judged, rejected, or betrayed.
- Will not meet with strangers, or try their best to avoid things like that.
- They seem reserved, introverted, or solitary due to the dread they feel when it comes to opening up to others.
- The overwhelming fear of being disappointed, or betrayed keeps them from having an intimate relationship.

If one has a problem with trusting others, it usually stems from being unable to trust oneself. This can greatly affect the intuition someone may have for dictating whether a person is trustworthy or not. Instead, everyone becomes untrustworthy which will greatly impact someone's life and choices.

People with Pistanthrophobia lack confidence in themselves. People who lack confidence think they are defenseless against others who attack them, hence becoming more distrustful. The phobia then cycles into a larger problem with this mindstate.

Having this phobia is like trying to climb a mountain when having vertigo. Building relationships become difficult because the fear of falling increases the steps you have to take, in which eventually you don't feel like you are moving forward anymore. Does this make sense?

This reason alone or overwhelming fear forces people to cut off relationships before they get too close. Again, much like people that have trust issues, the difference between the two is that Pistanthrophobia is an actual overwhelming, exaggerated fear of getting close to people, whereas having trust issues just alters your perspective of trust in yourself and others.

Chapter Three
Trust Issues in Relationships

"The best way to find out if you can trust somebody is to trust them" – Ernest Hemingway

We have been over the signs you may have trust issues. We have discussed what to look for in others. I explained the details in mind behind trust issues and where trust issues can come from. We have been over the topic of fear and what that is called, but now let's talk about relationships.

When people hear the word relationships, the first thing that usually comes to our mind is our partner or spouse. This is only one 'relationship' type I want to discuss. Relationships are everywhere; we make relationships with our parents, or friends, our family, our pets, and even strangers and co-workers.

Whether you don't trust your boss, a family member, a close friend, or strangers - it all boils down to why and where trust issues in these relations come from. We have already discussed the where, so let's dive a little deeper into the why. In order to do this, we must ask ourselves do we really know what trust is?

Well, here are my definitions:

What is Trust?

Trust is situation-specific. If we put our minds to this order of what trust is, then we can better understand the fundamentals on how to trust people, and let go of our trust issues. What I mean by trust being situation-specific, is that when we ask someone if they can do a task for you and they say they can but have no idea on how to do it, then they are setting you up to trust in the wrong person. Whereas, if they do have expertise in the task you are asking, there will be little room to break your trust, as they will know how to do the task you are asking of them. On the other hand, it doesn't just come down to if they have the expertise to do the task at hand.

When someone says 'I don't trust them,' this is making a statement based on opinion in which the person accused of being untrustworthy can do nothing about. This statement with no supporting evidence as to why is not helpful in building relationships when we believe the other person is the issue. When we believe that the source of the problem will be resolved when the other person makes a change, no good can come from this thought process.

When we understand that trust is situation-specific, we will then be able to build a better relationship with whom we want to trust. Example: Instead of saying "I don't trust them," we learn to say and think like this; "I trust so and so to be able to finish and deliver the task I have asked him or her to do, but I do not trust them to manage anything other than this." By minimizing trust down to situational aspects, you can further address how and why you trust or don't trust someone, which, in return, trains your brain that trust issues don't need to get out of hand.

Other than being situation-specific, there are other foundational components present to understand trust. These are known as the three

C's of trust and, without them, the thought behind trust falls apart, resulting in trust issues.

1. Competence

You trust someone to have the ability to do the task you are asking of them and it can be foolish of you to trust them to do so. Having the knowledge, skill, materials and the authority to complete a task is the base of trust.

2. Consistency

A person or organization may have the talent, experience, and expertise to do what is expected but, if their products are inconsistent, then this proves their credit to be low. If their credit rating to get jobs done on time is low, then we are automatically unable to put trust in them. We cannot depend on organizations or people if they have a history of uncompleted tasks or late payments.

3. Character

Character refers to honesty, credibility and the belief that the other person will take your needs as seriously as they would their own. In short, you need to know that the business or person you are dealing with is not going to become selfish due to keeping themselves afloat but also taking into consideration your needs alongside theirs.

In any relationships, it is best to keep the three C's in accordance with letting go of your trust. It is no wonder trust issues are popular in this modern day due to how many businesses and people are always looking to fraud, or betray easily. Again, trust issues only happen because of past experiences of trust being broken.

To set yourself up for having a healthy way to develop trust is to be logical with your trust without coming off as stingy or unwelcoming. The best ways to trust when in doubt is to keep these steps in mind:

- Which of the three C's is lacking or present in the business or personal arrangement you are about to make?

- Get them to explain all the details of your arrangement so you are on the same page, and no information is missed.

- Are there other variables in which would make it easier for you to trust this person or business (under supervision)?

- Give the person or business reasons to trust you, rather than no reasons to trust you - provide supporting evidence you can be trusted.

- Be willing to take other action to help them trust you as well.

- Live by the three C's. If you are going to expect someone else to follow the three C's, live by example by providing them yourself.

In order to live life in a co-operative fashion with anyone or any situation you face, trust in relationships is fundamental.

Reasons we May Find it hard to Trust the Ones we Love

Now that we have addressed and understood trust a little better, we can figure out what makes us reluctant to trust people, especially the ones we care so much about. The things we value the most come up in many situations in our lives that we rely on trusting strangers with. Example: Aspirations, hope, dreams, and desires rely solely on managers and employers for experience in the fields we would like to go into.

Vulnerabilities and opening up to colleagues that have seen us fail, we rely on these people to help us through and get ahead. Our own life may rely upon one stranger's hands as we walk the earth upon many strangers around us.

The common misconception people tend to make is trusting the ones we love the most, family members, spouses, parents, and children. The reason this is a misconception is that if we could trust the ones we love then why do teenagers give more trust to their friends talking about studies, relationships, emotions, and challenges of their own. Spouses can hide so much from one another being deceitful because they may feel weak or not good enough to their partner, which also comes down to trust and communication. A lot of us tend to put on a fake face in front of people we hang out with, all of, or most of the time, including our peers, cousins, and relatives. At the same time, why is it easier for most people to trust a complete stranger you share the same bus seat with rather than one closer to home?

Here are some reasons trust isn't easily given to the ones we love:

- **You may think they won't understand you**

This thought process is the reason children or young adults prefer to share with their friends or colleagues rather than parents or family; also, why adults refer to their friends rather than their spouses. The biggest reason we may feel our loved ones won't understand us is that they may have different views and perspectives. They may also be at a different stage in life as you, professionally and otherwise.

- **You may think you will be judged**

As everyone has an opinion - you may not be looking for one from a certain individual. Sharing your vulnerability, mistakes, mess or skeletons in the closet is not the easiest task to share with people who are closest to us. This comes from the fear that they will be judgmental of these attributes and secrets. Often families feel it is their duty to judge and label us - it is not okay, no matter who you are.

Family members or spouses may use your secrets against you during fights to hit you where it hurts the most, in which cases this can make someone bottle up and develop future trust issues. This is why we put on a fake mask to the ones we love as a coping mechanism to avoid being hurt by them.

In love, we try to search for unconditional acceptance. When we are in our darkest times or our weakest moments, that is when we seek their love and guidance the most. If we don't feel we are going to get this, but instead feel we will be judged, we will carry on portraying ourselves as happy, strong, and smart when, in reality, that is not the case.

- **You may feel whoever won't be able to handle the truth**

When we want to tell our loved ones personal things, we get scared of how they will react. Anger, shock, worry, sadness, and overwhelming emotions may all come from the other person, in which case if we are not prepared for their action, we set ourselves up for the development of trust issues. Our result is we hide what we want to or need to say because it is best not to trouble the other person.

Another worry of ours is that once we have told the individual what is important to us or what was on our minds, the individual may lack complete interest, be totally incoherent of it and start talking about themselves. Instead of listening to your feelings, they find a way to talk about their own in a similar situation of their own story. This is a major barrier in close relationships to open up to the other person.

- **Maybe you just have a general problem trusting anyone**

When this becomes a reason or an excuse, it doesn't have anything to do with the other person, but more on the inability to trust yourself. It is unwise to seek the decision that trust is based on trust alone, but it is not complete without fear. The opposite of trust is fear, not mistrust.

Constantly living in fear that something bad may happen or someone may betray you or hurt you, you will automatically trust less. To portray yourself as powerful, manipulating, menacing and hide information are all signs that you fear to trust and have little of it - trust issues.

Three positive things to take from this mindset is this:

1. It will be more helpful to understand why the other person can't trust us if that person has not been able to trust us with something. Creating an emotional outbreak will only add to the woes of that person and yourself.

2. Fear and suspicion should not hold us back from connecting new relationships and opportunities. If we continue to have trust issues in relationships around us, we will constantly miss out on the many great things our lives have to offer us. It is worth the risk of getting hurt, as long as many positive connections continue to happen for you.

3. Ever find yourself saying "If you hide things from me, that means you don't love me?" Well, one thing to get straight is that love and trust are far from being the same thing. Love does not cause trust and trust does not gain love. It is always our choice whether to trust the ones we love and, if we don't, then we find ways to fix it or move on.

Too many times I catch myself holding onto a friendship or a relationship out of the mere thought that they have the potential to change. I catch myself thinking just over this hill and things will be better. I just need to gain trust or be able to trust first and everything will be better. This is the wrong way to think. No trust means there is a lack of communication somewhere, whether that is in speech, body language or actions.

If you value the relationship at hand, you must first address where the trust issues are coming from. After this assessment, take a look at yourself - are you the cause of not being able to trust them, or are they the cause? Can this be fixed, dropped and moved on from, or is it going to drag your whole relationship down every step of the way towards your future? These are real questions to ask yourself when it comes to valuing yourself and someone else.

Trust Issues within a Friendship

Have you ever had a friend who went behind your back, or gossiped about you? Did you ever feel that maybe your close friend would be just that - a close friend – regardless of if you trust yourself, or never mind the fact that you may have trust issues about people around you. We never expect the closest people to us to betray us and make us feel unworthy, hence comes trust issues. If a friend breaks that, then you may feel like abandoning them or you may feel just plain spiteful against them. Regardless of how you feel, or what has happened, here are a few signs to watch out for if you suspect your friend may be becoming dishonest:

1. **They are undependable**

Any friend that has gained valuable trust will make sure that they can be depended on. Anytime you need someone, your friends are the ones you usually call, so do you have that one friend who says you can depend on them but fails to be there when you need them? Dependable friends are ones who can be reliable when you need an outlet or someone to hear you vent. If they fail to do so, your trust flag may be raised.

However, just because you can't depend on them doesn't necessarily mean they can't be trusted, it just means that you are most likely going to feel more skeptical of them.

2. They fail to compromise with you

In every relationship, whether it is with your boss, a co-worker, or your husband, there has to be compromise. Well, the same goes for a friend. According to John Gottman, author of *The Science Of Trust,* over time, trust is built; meaning gradually through any relationship trust between two people or more increases. To compromise means to put someone else's happiness above yours, or come to some sort of middle ground if you can't agree.

3. They have inconsistent behavior

Suspicions may come to mind when a friend of yours has changeable behavior. Someone who is all over the place and constantly busy who cannot make time for your needs regularly may seem untrustworthy. This is not to say they can't be trustworthy as a person but as a friend.

Of course, people have lives, and people are going to be busy, but that doesn't mean they can't pick up the phone and call you at the end of the day. Inconsistent behavior means to not follow through with a routine so, as your friend may be consistent with other duties in his/her life, they may fail to interact with you and their behavior may seem untrustworthy.

4. They make excuses to cancel constantly

An important trait or quality we look for in friends is how reliable they are or can be - the ability to keep plans. The sense of trust diminishes when we are left behind, or waiting around for someone who promises to show up. If you have a friend who makes promises and keeps them, you are most likely going to continue to grow the trust between you. If you have a friend who makes you feel less than important, well, obviously your trust for them is going to turn into trust issues for later when they actually mean what they say. It comes down to credibility making plans and sticking with them.

5. They like to gossip

Say you are hanging out with a friend, and all they can do is talk about others, or vent about other people's secrets, you guys have a great conversation and they leave. Then, when the next time you hang out, they do it again, maybe about the same person and maybe about someone else. After this becomes a regular thing, you have to wonder if they may be talking about you to others as well. If you get the sense they could be talking about you, your gut may be right and it is best to listen to it. The friends to look for are the ones who want to talk about their own life, or they are more interested in talking about yours. Topics of other people should not come up, but only occasionally according to your current topic.

Not only will your friend talk about other people, but the things he/she is telling you may be confidential to someone else, so how can you trust them with your own secrets. You should definitely be aware of friends that gossip about you.

6. They flirt with your boyfriend, or someone you are interested in

Everyone has friend codes that should not be crossed. Some people may have more or fewer codes than another friend may have. One thing is always dominant when it comes to friendship – leave the boyfriend or person of interest alone.

I am not saying you can't have them be friends with your man (or woman), but for them to get strangely closer and closer to your spouse or person of interest should shoot a red flag. Also, if you introduce your friend to your person, then you are already putting trust in your friend not to cross that line. This is tricky though if your man/woman entices your friend to be friendlier without your knowledge. If this happens, then maybe you should be looking for another person to spend your life with as well. In the same sentence, if your friend was trustworthy, he or she should or would shoot your partner down with any type of flirting going on.

7. Most of the time they lie

The obvious point I am here to make is when your friend continues to lie, or be dishonest, or have dishonest-like actions. I hope that all the other points I have made were a clear enough sign that this should be the tell-tale sign. If your friend has done all of these or some of these things, then without me telling you, you are probably having some trust issues with them already.

Everyone lies from time to time, whether they are exaggerating a story or undermining the truth, whether they are hiding from the truth or avoiding it - the point is everyone lies. The big difference about when you should or may have trust issues with a friend is if they constantly lie, especially when the lies are spinning out of control and you hear a different story about it the next time they tell you, or if it's not little lies anymore.

In conclusion to the 7 signs described above, this is not to say that because of these signs, your friend shouldn't be trusted and you should push them out of your life. If you have any suspicions about it, you should simply just sit them down and talk to them about your worries. My advice is to not trust them any further until you can sit down and discuss their behavior and actions towards your friendship bond. Also, trust goes both ways, so if any of these signs remind you of yourself with someone else, the best bet would be to talk to them too if you value or want to keep that friend near.

Reasons you are Unable to Trust Your Boss

Aside from having your own trust issues within yourself, you need to ask yourself in every situation if it's you with the trust issue, or if someone has given you a reason to not trust them. The times where trust issues become a problem is when you excessively go out of your way to not trust someone regardless of if you have reasons to believe otherwise or not.

Many times an employer would take great measures to make sure the person they hired could be trusted. A lot of times it was hard to tell based on many employees lying about their skills and work ethic on their resumés. Recently, tables have seemed to turn. Employees are now finding it difficult to truth their bosses, and for a good reason. Here are a few factors explaining why:

1. **Lack of engagement**

The lack of engagement in the work field results in a loss of trust. We also see this in other interpersonal relationships. When an employee is disengaged and the employer lacks to improve it, it risks billions of dollars to the company. Employee engagement is classified as a strong emotional and intellectual connection that an employee has for their job, organization, and manager, thus resulting in high-quality work performance. If the employer does not make this connection, then it won't matter how much the employee loves their line of work, as engagement is a must!

2. Temporary thinking

Temporary thinking, also known or preferred as short-term thinking, is when a company thinks about the short-term goals for themselves, rather than long-term survival for the organization. Employees find it hard to trust any boss or business they work for if they feel the business isn't set up for sticking around for a long time. With this state of mind, companies will often end up losing potential long-term employees because the employee will want to grow with a business, rather than feel like they are being someone to step on, so the business can get ahead.

If a business took more time to get to know their employees, and what the employee needs, the employee will likely be willing to stay as they will feel beneficial to the business. For a company to set only small goals, it means they are looking to complete the small goals at a time, just keeping the business afloat. Making long-term goals means better business and long-term employees who they can trust.

It's like a house! A house can have people live in it, go to work from it and come home to it every night, but a house is much different than a home. If the people inside the housework together every day to keep it clean and raise a family for many years to come with add-ons and events, then the property value raises, therefore, making profit and trust within the home.

3. A non-believer of the company

People want to work for employers who are addressing every need of their growing business. This means looking after their employees and protecting the environment around the workspace or the company. Employees like to communicate with employers who believe in what they are saying, and act accordingly to their beliefs. After all, if an employer isn't interested in making the company strive, how can an employee trust that they are in the right hands?

4. Poor quality product

Do you want to work for a company that sells great products and works well with people around them? Well, often, there are times an employer falls short of completing these simple tasks. Employers are supposed to lead by example. If the employer invests in selling high-quality products while presenting a great service, the employee is going to trust that their boss knows what to do, and will follow their lead.

It is always easier to work for a company that will put pride into their products and consumers. If an employee can choose to support the employer's products personally, then it is easy to put their trust in the company they work for. If an employee is constantly answering calls to angry customers, then the toll it will take on an employee will drag them down, and eventually, they will grow onto another business that actually takes pride, rather than listening to angry customers every day.

5. Dishonorable behavior

When a company is dishonorable or shady, the employee is going to have difficulty trusting the company. Dishonorable behavior means that the business is not cleaning up after themselves, and earning a massive amount of money at the expense of others. A business that is using people to get ahead is a business bound to fail - this is unethical.

If a business doesn't set a good example for themselves, then they don't set good examples of their employees. Employees trust companies that will take the time to do things by the book and get ahead. An employer will trust a company more if they have reason to grow with the business or organization.

6. Bad credibility

Before starting a job, what employees look for are things like good ratings and positive reviews about working for the business. It is stressful enough finding work or coming into a new environment, along with having to support your own life with a steady financial income.

If a company does not deliver a consistent financial return and has a poor leadership team, it will be close to impossible to attract loyal and trusting employees. People hate working for businesses that are known for their negative attribute or have low work environment ratings.

7. Non-existent boss

A non-existent boss is a boss that shows he or she doesn't care. If a boss doesn't care, then why should the employee? Without being able to discuss financial results or societal issues, it becomes hard for the employee to trust and know what the company is about.

8. Lack of communication

A boss that does not communicate with the employees on a regular, if not weekly basis, will leave employees in the dark wondering and having questions unanswered; thus, leaving unfinished work or even non-existent employees. Communication is key in every relationship, but when it comes to working, things get real heavy real quickly if a discussion does not take place.

Communication within a company is not just about talking; it consists of appointments and business meetings. It also consists of building an environment outside of the workplace, such as in newsletters, industry conferences, and/or website updates etc. Without this much-needed communication process, the trust between employee and employer becomes almost invisible.

Trusting a business can be hard, but trusting an employee can have the same amount of difficulty. It takes work, leadership, experience, and dedication on everyone's part to make and grow an uplifting, supportive workplace. If an employee does not work to the best of their ability, it can come down to how the business decides to operate. If a business does not strive to be the best it can be for growth, then it can simply come down to the employees it has, and their determination to working hard.

Signs that Trust Issues are Affecting Your Marriage

Many people have trust issues. Trust issues stem from a lot of things, one being in particular with the past. Past childhood abuse or neglect can raise having difficulties with trusting someone, but that mainly results in a lack of confidence and trust in yourself. The other form of trust issue you may experience is if you have had a past with untrustworthy spouses, or even had events happen in your current relationship that causes you to have a hard time trusting your partner.

The question to ask yourself is this: "Do I have trust issues, or am I genuinely concerned about if my spouse can be trusted?" Also, what is the difference between the two? So, if you are sitting there constantly on edge and thinking about what your partner may be doing or not doing, ask yourself if you have done this in past relationships as well. If you have, then you are the common denominator. The best way to figure this out is to search inside yourself, and figure out exactly where these trust issues are coming from, and try to understand exactly where and how they came about.

Still, need help? Here is a list I have provided with signs you may be the problem.

1. **You freeze in most situations**

As a form of a coping mechanism, you shut down in front of your partner with certain topics like talking about the past or the future. Although it feels inevitable to stop this from happening, you also struggle with understanding why this happens. A dating coach, Nora Dekeyser, says "Communication is key when you freeze up. Linking it to something that happened in the past will help you both to figure out where this trust issue is coming from. Separately, work on this within yourself, and understand that this pain is not in your current relationship, but in your past ones." If it helps, let your partner in on what you are going through so they can be as supportive as they can for you.

2. **You get triggered easily - with no explanation**

When you feel yourself becoming emotional and vulnerable but don't understand why, it may be because something that was said or done has triggered you. This is an important moment because it gives you an opportunity to channel this feeling to anything that may have stemmed from your past. If it has, then you know it could be something else and not your partner.

Dekeyser says, "Our subconscious can make us think we are in control when the truth is we are not, our actions are being controlled subconsciously without realizing it at first. There are some tools like meditation, mindfulness, and self-awareness to help you work through triggers so that when something happens, you are not triggered anymore." Of course, that takes lots of practice and dedication, but if you want to work through this, you can and you will.

3. You push your partner away

Often, if the trust issues are something that only you are going through and you have clear signs that you aren't just genuinely concerned but have extreme problems with trust, you will push the other person away. Whether this is on purpose or by accident, you still manage to push them away. The reason you push them aside is mostly that you don't want to hurt them, and you don't want to be hurt - again, a coping mechanism to help yourself.

Be careful when you push someone away. If you keep that at a steady length, where only you can put up or down your walls at any given time, you and your spouse will lack connection. Lacking connection will not only hurt them, but it will hurt you as well. There is only so much one can take as well when you push them aside.

4. You find yourself spying on them

If you find yourself extremely suspicious to the point of having to snoop through your partner's emails and text messages with no reason to do so, that is a definite sign your past relationships could be triggering your current one. Also, in many places, a breach of someone's privacy is illegal, and you are taking chances of being reported by your spouse, which can turn into very ugly situations.

5. You panic

Are you constantly catastrophizing everything? Do you think the worst when your partner leaves the house? Are you constantly questioning them when they aren't around - and then question yourself as to why? This is a major result of trust issues. Because of what happened to you in the past, you feel the need to be constantly reassured. Due to this questioning, over-analyzing attitude, you may feel like your relationship is falling apart and you often wonder why. You may feel like it really isn't your fault.

In these moments, breathe. Give your partner the benefit of the doubt, regardless of if anything had happened between you two or someone from your past. Over-estimating the time it takes to get from your house to the store and back again may just be that a train had stopped them on the way and he/she really is just five minutes late.

6. You think it is necessary to breach your partner's trust

If you are in a mindset that something will go wrong because every relationship goes wrong, that is proof you have deep issues to work on within yourself. As long as you continuously think that everyone cheats and lies, or that your spouse will never be able to make up for what they have done in the past, then your relationship will continue to be on the rocks and, eventually, you will end up alone. You don't want to be alone, and you don't deserve to be either.

7. You feel uncontrollable

Are you going through this list of the past six things, and you feel yourself say "Yep, yep, yep?'" At the same time, you are sitting here and thinking "How do I stop? What do I do? And why do I do this?" These are true signs that the trust issues you have are taking over you and they are taking over your love life. This needs to stop and, later in this book, I will explain how. The fact that you are aware of these signs and still don't know how to stop it, shows that you are struggling and you are bringing the ones you love down with you too.

In conclusion, understanding and accepting that you have a trust issue is the first step to getting better. Getting better is not going to happen overnight, and you won't get better unless you actually want to. Now that you have it, maybe you are thinking to yourself "In time, if my spouse or partner doesn't do anything, and I am always proven wrong, then my trust issues will go away, and there will be no problems" - WRONG!

Even if that mindset made sense and, in a perfect world that actually happened, your relationship wouldn't last very long after because behaving like the steps above will only happen for so long until your partner either leaves you, or you transfer your trust issues onto them. You may feel fine in a year or two, but with the amount of time it takes to continue this process, the eggshells your spouse is walking on can hurt their mental state. Don't be selfish – go and get help.

Learning How to Trust Your New Spouse

It is okay to be skeptical when getting to know someone new. Be grateful that you got yourself back out there in the dating world, as someone with trust issues finds it very difficult to continue with intimacy. The question is - are you ready to trust again? In your past relationships, you may have been betrayed or lied to, but one thing to keep in mind is that you will be able to trust again. With the right action, steps, and patience with yourself, you can get back on track.

Kayla Knopp, a clinical graduate student says, "To trust is a decision, not a feeling." If you feel like your past relationships are 'baggage' or that maybe you will never be able to trust someone again, be reassured because the reality is that your experiences can be used productively for your future. Here is a list of tips and tactics to get your head on straight for your new partner:

- **Change your frame of mind**

Don't think of your experiences as baggage. Every failed attempt at anything in life is a reason to create success for your future. It is best to be honest with your fresh partner about things that concern you, boundaries not to cross and experiences you have been through. Choosing when to have this talk is probably best before any sexual relations. Get to know them first before diving in if you truly want to succeed.

If you are honest with yourself as well as your new spouse, this will create a whole line of communication you and your exes maybe didn't have. It is best to be realistic in this case because you want to try to avoid letting the pain from the past interfere with the potential happiness you could have now. Becoming jealous and asking for too much reassurance at the start of something great can turn into the end of the great thing quicker than you would imagine.

- **Separate your past from your present and future**

People tend to make their current partner feel like they need to pay for their past partner's misdeeds. It is good and always necessary to remember that your current lover is not your ex, nor will they ever be, so calm down. Try this exercise – create a split-screen in your mind between the ex and the current, and compare the evidence of trustworthiness between the two. Has your new partner done anything to make you feel you can't trust them? Other than your own beliefs, and imaginations you dream up, what is your current partner doing, or not doing, that your ex did? If there are little things like your current relationship often checks their phone or walks away with it when they talk, don't automatically think they are doing what your ex did. Give them the benefit of the doubt. Understand that they are not your past and hopefully they won't be.

- **Identify patterns**

Ever wonder why you are sticking around with the same person even though everything in you shouts to leave? That is because our brains are wired to seek out what is familiar and stay with it even when we don't realize it. If you find yourself in this 'love trap,' consider looking back at healthy relationships like your parents or people you know.

Understanding patterns within yourself and others will help you clarify what is best for your needs and theirs. It is best to stay selfless rather than selfish; realizing that things that didn't work for you in the past will not work for you now. Remember that doing the same thing you have always done won't change your future but, instead, will keep you repeating your patterns.

- **Define whether they are worth your trust**

Get to know the new person well before jumping in. Are they worthy of the trust you want to give them? People tend to take others for granted. Keep in mind that everyone has a dark side and that some people may use you to gain trust just to do deceitful things behind your back later. When you are getting involved with someone new, make sure you know them before continuing to create a life with them. If you don't, you may be looking at new patterns starting and setting your future up unsuccessfully.

- **Have an unbiased opinion**

Going into a new situation unbiased will shed light on your new beginning. You must not judge yourself, or your new spouse. It is always best to understand your new potential partner so that you know most about them, and they know most about you as well. If you want a fair shot at love, try looking at this new situation as if you have never 'been there and done that.' Pretend you are a new employee being trained on how to do everything from the start.

So, with this in mind, when you start to look for a new 'job,' you look for things like experience, leadership, rankings, professionalism, and ways to grow. Treat the new partner like this as if you were looking for a new job. Now, you have picked the career you want, but why? Think about your new partner in an unbiased and objective view; look for the people they hang around with, and what are they like. Look at their family and interpret how they treat each other. How does your spouse treat the ones they care about? Look at their profession, their kids, their influences, and their attitudes. What are their best and worst qualities? What do their friends say about them? These are all things to look for when being with someone new without being biased upon your past. If this person is worthy of your trust, then the answers you search won't be hard to find.

- **Communicate in a humble way**

As every relationship has the 'ex-talk,' figuring out when to do so is the most difficult aspect of a new relationship. One thing to keep in mind when this happens, or for any important future topic, is to listen to understand, don't listen to respond. It is good to open up to them about what is going on with you, while, at the same time, keeping an open mind for when they want to talk.

If, however, they are listening to respond and only talk about themselves whilst not hearing you, this could be a 'red flag' that communication is maybe not their strong point. Also, understand that there are three sides to every story and what they tell you may not be the whole truth but their perspective of the truth. That doesn't mean they are lying; it means they speak based on what they experienced.

- **Trust yourself**

Many times, through bad experiences, we wonder if we were ever good enough or going to be. We beat ourselves up for missing clear and definite signs, or maybe we did see it but expected it to change as it never did. When we love someone, we tend to give them too many chances while letting ourselves continue to feel and be betrayed. Within this comes the difficulty to trust ourselves.

If this sounds like you, then the best thing you can do is address this with your new relationship. Having strong communication with your partner, especially in the beginning, can set your relationship up for continued success along the way. If your partner is willing to support you, and help you explore your doubt without sounding too pushy, then you will feel a sense of safety together which, in return, is a healthy relationship finally.

- **Expect negative emotions**

No-one is perfect and so be sure to make room for mistakes - for yourself and your spouse. With problems with trust, you are bound to fall off the perfect track record you have been managing so far with occasional thoughts of doubt, worry, and jealousy. This is understandable considering your previous experiences.

The best thing to do is to give yourself time and patience. Be careful not to blame your partner for how you feel. Guide your actions and decisions by your values instead of your fear.

- **Make your expectations known**

As I have said before, communication is key, so communicating with your partner about what you expect, along with keeping a non-judgmental tone, is the best thing to do when entering something new. When you have the 'ex-talk,' be sure to mention what was done, and how it made you feel. Be sure to ask them if they have ever been through the same thing or something similar. As you have this talk, the conclusion of your discussion should have a solution. The best solution to consider is clearing up how one of you will deal with it if any of you were to experience feelings for someone else in the future. By doing this, the hope is to avoid future uncomfortable situations.

- **Therapy can help**

If you are still struggling with trust issues, talking to a therapist can help and may greatly improve all relationships in your life. Many times, the experiences we have gone through are just too traumatizing to move forward with our lives, so a little help from a professional is a great idea.

A therapist can help you with coping strategies and give you daily tasks to work on as you manage your trust issues. They can give you the advice you have never heard of, and they are there to help you with your individual needs for your situation.

- **Understand the risks you are taking**

Be open-minded and patient with yourself. The only person who has to live with you is yourself. Don't judge yourself or reflect too much on what has happened. Try to let go and move on what was not healthy and look forward to what will be. This may be difficult to do when your heart has been broken to the point of 'no return.'

Before letting someone in, it is natural to feel like you'll never be able to open your heart again. Due to protecting yourself, your thoughts may sound something like *"Will I ever be able to trust again? Can I take the risk of being hurt if it happens again? What will I do if the past repeats itself?"* These are all normal thoughts, but, whatever you do, do not carry them with you into your new relationship. We, as humans, fear the unknown and are most of the time scared to take the jump that leads us to the next step. Well, most of the time any risk is worth taking because you can walk away learning something or continue growing into the person you are meant to be.

Chapter Four
Dealing With Trust Issues

"Trust should be earned and only with the passage of time" – Arthur Ashe

Having trust issues come from past violence, relationship issues, broken trust, constant feelings of betrayal, and being nurtured into being a cautious, skeptical person. It is okay to be cautious and, most times skepticism is a good thing, but unhealthy behaviors such as looking over your shoulder, thinking others will constantly let you down, being extremely wary that your neighbors are up to no good, and always being on guard can really start to control your life. Sometimes, as we have learned, this can happen even when we don't want it to. Learning how to deal with these problems is of utmost importance if you want to lead a happy influential journey.

Signs You Don't Trust Yourself

Before we can dive into how to deal with your trust issues within yourself and other aspects of your life, we must first find the signs and reasons about trusting yourself. Good instincts and support will help you start to grow as an individual and get out of this slump you are in. Self-trust is one of the first steps to work on before working on trusting anyone else. The same goes for love - if you can't trust yourself, then how do you expect to trust anyone else? Here is a list of signs you potentially don't trust yourself:

1. You may have a hard time recognizing and believing in yourself

and your worth.

2. Your childhood may have been filled with negative self-rejecting messages from your peers.

3. You believe there is something that could have been done about your abusive childhood but didn't do it.

4. You constantly look for reassurance in yourself from others.

5. As a coping mechanism, you protect yourself by controlling everything around you.

6. You second-guess your decisions based on the influences in your life. You are questioning if you are doing or living appropriately by comparing yourself to others.

7. You often don't feel like your needs are good enough to address.

8. You shut down in front of others because you are not confident enough to have, or find, your own voice.

9. You escape the truth or run from telling it. Sometimes, you don't tell the full truth as a protection from getting hurt.

10. Negative self-talk becomes your life. Negative behaviors and beliefs about yourself become a habit.

11. You are always quick to think that you will get hurt or someone will disappoint you if you get close to them. You fear betrayal.

12. You constantly beat yourself up or create dilemmas inside your head that create strong overwhelming feelings of shame, guilt, and self-punishment.

13. Promises are broken within yourself and others.

14. You don't finish what you start.

15. You find yourself thinking about bad things and holding grudges against people who have hurt or harmed you.

16. You constantly listen to others' advice, letting them control your life without thinking about it as a step towards reassurance.

17. You don't make decisions based on intuition, instincts, and inner guidance, but rather go against them in hopes of proving yourself wrong.

If any of the above sounds like you, then you are on the right track by continuing to read more of the book and how to help yourself. This behavior is very unhealthy and can lead to depression and other disorders. Together, let's make the steps to recovery and get you to find confidence within yourself.

How to Take Hold of Your Trust Issues

For a long time now you have known you have trust issues. You have read, researched, and tried to fix the problem, but nothing seems to work. The problem isn't with the information you hold; it is within yourself. You must first accept that you have a problem; from there the rest is a constant uphill battle of getting better.

It's like anxiety. I have an anxiety disorder, and I manage it day in and day out. I have gone to counseling and I know everything I should know about it. For a while, I was not getting anywhere. I tried coping methods and counseling. I tried eating better and thinking better. Nothing seemed to work because I didn't accept that I had it. With anxiety though, much different from having trust issues, you have to let it in. Let the anxiety take over, and be okay with that. Understand that once you acknowledge something, it can't control you anymore.

With having trust issues, I would imagine doing the opposite of what your thoughts tell you to do is key. Accept that you have difficulty trusting people and yourself. Acknowledge that it is going to take hard work to get better. Unlike anxiety, the good news is that if you work at being able to trust yourself and others every day, one day you will just wake up and not be as bad as you were, to then eventually not having a struggle with it anymore. Wouldn't that be nice? Here is one of the first steps:

1. **Accept the 'danger' that comes with learning to trust again**

If you tell yourself that you can and will trust again, you will. You must believe to achieve. Again, no-one is perfect and everyone lets someone down, whether they mean to or not. If you accept that in order to trust again, you will be let down at one point or another, it's inevitable and cannot be avoided.

Learning to trust again takes guidance, control, confidence, and hard work. Believe that you are good enough the way that you are and don't let anyone change that. As long as you are stuck with the mindset that once trust is broken it can't be regained or rebuilt, you are setting yourself up for failure. The goal is to get away from this negative thinking and onto more important things in life.

Even if you don't trust people or yourself, it doesn't mean you don't trust at all. When you go to a restaurant, you 'trust' that they won't poison you; when you got to a job interview, you 'trust' that the employer knows what he is talking about. Your brain naturally wants to trust, so let it in.

Listen to your instincts. This is a big one because there are often times we try to go against them and then get proven wrong, or get betrayed because we didn't listen to our inner voice. Look at yourself in a mirror and tell yourself that you deserve love and a healthy, functioning brain. Your worth is valuable, so don't let anyone take that from you. Also, mindfulness and meditation can greatly improve the trust you feel inside yourself. Paying attention to yourself and your cues will make for great accomplishments later in life.

2. Research about trust and how it works

Read this book and then read it again. If you want a second opinion, research on the Internet or in books of 'how to's' and 'definitions of.' This will help you get a better sense of what you are dealing with. Before just giving out your trust to anyone, first, make sure you trust yourself to make the call on if someone is worthy of your trust or not. Also, it is good to keep in mind that you cannot give trust unless you are willing to accept the trust. Just don't give too much and don't expect too much more in return.

3. Take emotional adventures

To take on an emotional risk, would be to let go of your fear for taking such risks. Not a task people normally agree to. Taking these adventures means to let someone else 'walk in your shoes,' and by them being able to do that, means you may have to open up and let them know what's happening in your life. This is another thing that millions of people are not okay with, so you are not alone.

If you want to take emotional risks, you have to do and be okay with four things, doing which involves hands, thinking which involves your head, feeling which involves your heart and being which involves your gut. You must use every ounce or part of your body to commit to taking such risks. When your body says no, push because you know you can.

When you do something, it sets the ball in action. When you think about things, it will define how you act or react during your life - think positive, live positive, think negative, live negative. When you open your heart to feel, it means to share your feelings and express those emotions. If you don't at least try, loneliness and bitterness will become you. Your gut consists of the overall strength and feeling you have about a situation. It also consists of the way you feel about yourself or someone else - the deepest level of connection a person can feel.

4. Face the unknown and the negatives that involve trust

When you stare fear in the face, fear backs off. This is true because I have lived it, and I live it every day, being an anxiety victim. The first step to facing your fear is to ignore what your negative thoughts tell you. When you listen to your demons, they become a part of you. The goal is to block them out so you can be happier with the steps you take moving forward. Demons make you second- guess, angels point you on the right path.

When you fall back into your patterns, and that little voice inside your head tries to convince you that you are being betrayed or set up to be hurt, don't ignore it, challenge it. As long as you give in to these thought patterns and the traps of distrust, you will always have a safety net to return to and therefore trust controls you. If we want to reach our goals, we must first ignore the traps our brain sets for us because they will only try to stop us from achieving our needs.

When your instincts scream at you to run, you run. When your emotions are telling you to fall, you fall. When your brain tells you this feels right or doesn't feel right, listen to it. Without second-guessing everything built inside of you to help you strive, feel your feelings. Take on those crazy emotions and let them in. As scary as this sounds, you can do it.

If that didn't sound scary, then this will: be vulnerable and open. People turn away from being or doing these two things because they are scared of getting hurt. Well, as explained before, it is inevitable, and you will not be able to go your whole life avoiding hurt when it is bound to happen, so stop trying to run from it. If you are honest with yourself, then the rest will come easily.

5. Try to trust again - eventually, you will

If you follow the last four steps, then you are on the road to success. Live by these rules and trust will come slowly but surely for you again. The truth is you can't run from pain as it will just catch up on you. You can't avoid feeling betrayed and hurt as that is a part of what makes us humans. When you learn to do the opposite of your triggers and understand that it is okay to have difficulties with trust, you will see that the world will start to open up again. Don't ignore these opportunities ahead. Don't let trust issues control you and the people around you. Remember that you deserve a better life, not an ugly one full of regret.

Chapter Five
Fixing the Problem

"Trust yourself, you know more than you think you do" - Benjamin Spock

Now that we have learned almost everything about trust and trust issues, it is time to dive into fixing the problems. When someone has trust issues, their world revolves around the stories they dream up in their head that isn't even real or true. They think they know the full story because the part of the brain that thinks logically (as explained previously) stops working. Our brains have a hard time filing trust and trust issue scenarios because they are one in the same.

One thing to know for sure is if you have a hard time trusting people, the best thing to do about it is to get better. Let go of the blame, let go of the past, let go of the problems that arise around the trust issue, and just sit and think about what you are doing to yourself, and the ones you love. If you don't manage to fix the problem, then it's no wonder you push people away because you are tired of hurting them and yourself. Without solving the root problems to your trust issues, others will eventually start pushing you away too. As exhausting as it is for you to live this life, imagine how difficult it must be on your relationships with the people around you too.

Overcoming Trust Issues in a Partnership

Let's start with intimate relationships. The fact about having a difficult time to trust your partner is that the longer you act in the skeptical, suspicious way, the more you are hurting the relationship. Yes, it goes both ways because as long as the other half acts and does things that are disloyal or untrustworthy, then you have reason to be skeptical. The bottom line is that no matter how you look at it, the problem all goes back to having trust issues. Here are just a few pointers to help you gain some insight on ways to make a change for a healthier partnership.

- **Don't let it consume you**

What I mean by this is, don't let the issues take control of you. When you start thinking "What is he/she doing?"; "Why hasn't she/he texted me back?"; "They must be doing something to hurt me or betray me because it was bound to happen and that is what everyone does." When these thoughts start to spiral out of control, the worst thing to do is be stuck in them. By listening to these thoughts, you are feeding these fears and giving in to the insecurity that you feel.

Instead, what you can do, or try to do, is just notice the thought is there and distract your mind with something else. Before picking up the phone and asking every question in the book to your lover, sit down and read a book, play a game, or talk to someone else. Actually, maybe talking to someone other than your spouse, like a friend, about what you want to do right now and it feels almost impossible not to, your friend may have some really good advice. However, make sure this friend of yours is a positive non-judgmental friend who doesn't dislike the other person; otherwise, they will just be feeding you with new inventive things to say once your partner walks through the door.

When you let this feeling of betrayal and past patterns overtake you, your fear wins. You are no longer in control of how you feel, what you want, or even how to think. When this happens and you give into these untrustworthy feelings you are having, the logical thinking part of your brain turns off because now all you feel is fear, anger, sadness, and resentment. How can you fix things or think rational when your emotions take over? So, the next time this happens, don't let it consume you - breathe and distract yourself. Let the feeling pass and, if it still bothers you later, address it with your spouse when you have thought about every angle of the emotion and situation.

- **Talk to your partner about the distrust you have**

I can't stress this enough - COMMUNICATION IS FUNDAMENTAL. If you have a hard time communicating with your partner, find a mediator or get a therapist to help out. When you address the reasons you may be having difficulties trusting them, they may be able to pinpoint why and, if not, maybe they will try to understand. Whether or not you think they understand or don't, realize that you cannot do more than just talking to them.

Be careful about the words you use and the tone you have when talking to your partner. The last thing you would want to do is make them feel cornered or attacked. If things get heated, walk away and come back to it later, or find a different way to get your point across. If you have to tell a mutual friend so that they can help, or if you have to write it down, whatever the case, make sure your partner gets the message.

When discussing these issues you feel with them, understand that just telling them you don't trust them isn't going to solve anything. You have to think about the five W's that you learned in elementary school. The who, what, where, when, and why. When you explain in full detail your concerns and how you feel while keeping a positive, calm tone, the conversation will be more successful. After you explain, ask them to repeat back to you how they interpreted your explanation so you both can be on the same page. Once they have done this, wait for them to process and think about it (this may take a day or two). After you feel you have been patient enough, re-address the talk in brief later and see if they have come up with a solution to help you with this.

The goal is to come to a common ground and remember to compromise and sacrifice. If you put in 100% of yourself to everyone, they will most likely reciprocate that to you. If they don't, then maybe it is time to start thinking about other options for your relationship to be healthy - living apart or living together. Another tip is to make sure you or the people stay away from blaming one another. If they say you are being irrational, accept it and swallow it but also understand that two people don't think the same and so, more than likely, they don't perceive what you see. Fix it, don't run from it or avoid it.

- **Give them a chance to rebuild**

This may be hard to do, but with the trust issues that you already have, you are bound to think they can never be trusted again. In some ways you are right, but it is not right to let this thought consume you. One thing to realize is that once trust is broken, it can be hard to give your partner the benefit of the doubt in the hopes they won't hurt you again - unless they never have and this stems from the past.

If you want to make things work and you want things to be better, you have to give them a chance to make things work also. Trust is hard to fix, but it is not impossible. After giving time and space from each other, re-evaluate how you feel about them and what life is like with them (when it was good) and without them. If it is harder to be apart, then you know your answer - you want to make it work.

Once you come back to each other, let them show you, you have nothing to worry about. While working on your own skills in not letting your thoughts and fears take over, show them that you are willing to trust them again. This is not to constantly blame, and ask questions constantly though. Remember a healthy relationship takes effort, time, patience and never giving up on the other. Constantly trying to make it work is exhausting, but if you want it bad enough, then you must do whatever it takes.

- **You can't drive somebody to act a specific way**

The first step is letting yourself and them conclude that things need to be made right again. Understand that you are not them and so you don't think the way they do and vice versa. Understand that in time if things were meant to be right, they will be. Everyone has different ways of looking at things, for example, different point of views, different perspectives, and different behaviors and attitudes. You can't expect them to do exactly as you would in their shoes because the truth is you are not in their shoes and they are not in yours.

Although you can try to rebuild the trust and you can try to help them understand, sometimes what you want is not what you get. Be okay with this thought. Try gaining the perspective that things don't always go as planned and we are people. People make mistakes all the time and dragging it on will only break what you have further, rather than connect you more.

- **Just do and be who you are**

This may sound selfish but doing you is the best thing for your soul. If your soul is not happy, then how can you expect yourself or anyone around you to be. If you know who you are, then be just that - who you are. If you don't know who you are, then maybe some soul searching will be good for you. Know your worth and don't be fazed by the things you can't change or control. As long as you have tried and continue to try at everything you achieve and do, then that is all you should expect from yourself.

How to Overcome Trust Issues

If we don't learn how to overcome the trust issues that break us down inside, we will not learn how to unblock ourselves from letting the good things in life happen. Many experiences in our lives prevent us from being able to trust people and situations around us. If we have been raised with a rough childhood (as previously explained), then it is even harder for us to grow and develop into the people we are meant to be.

One of the first steps to healing is to figure out the depth of the wound and where it came from. Chelli Pumphrey, a therapist, suggests that you have to 'identify the origin of the wound that caused the trust issues. She says there are two types of trust issues, general trust issues that build over time and the deeper wounds that result to fear others.

The general type that builds over time consists of feelings of betrayal brought on by others' deceitful actions. The deeper kind that causes fear consists of abuse such as physical, sexual, emotional, and/or any traumatic experience that leads to an extreme lack of trust in other people, yourself and life. Due to these kinds of experiences, the brain can become wired to react in fear and irrational thoughts, with any trigger due to the past pain or trauma. Even when you don't mean to, you push people away or keep a 'safe' distance as a protective measure. Other times, you may be doing the exact opposite and trust everyone too much, even when your instincts scream at you not to. This type of trust issue often requires professional help within the mental health field.

Consider these few tactics to move forward with your life and open up to people:

- **Rewrite your story**

You have the right to take back your life. You can't control other people, and you can't control situations that happen in your lifetime, but you can control how you feel and what you think about it. By feeling angry and hurt, it is easy to feel like you are being victimized and build walls to protect yourself. As long as you stay in this rut or unhealthy thinking pattern, your pain will intensify and you will continue to be stuck in the trap your mind wants you to stay in. Look for the positive in every situation. Even when you don't see it, there is always a positive way on the most negative experiences. The heart only becomes stronger the more you use it, so embrace vulnerability and get comfortable with taking risks.

- **Embrace vulnerability**

Imagine holding your breath for a long period of time, or diving underwater. The air that you can't grasp for is slowly hurting your lungs and, if you hold it for too long, you start to lose control and slowly die due to suffocation. Finally, you reach towards the surface and gasp for air, your lungs become full of oxygen, your muscles relax and your mind is set to ease that you get to live one more moment. Trust is no different than this.

It is human nature to trust and love rather than succumb to the feelings of fear. When we are born, we naturally want to love automatically. Only when the experiences in our lives create fear and loss of control do we learn to distrust and have negative emotions. Fear is good to have in situations like not putting our hands on an open flame, or not to walk into traffic, or don't walk down an alley alone in the dark. This fear is good for survival and it's called common sense, but then there is fear that is created from unreal stories we dream up in our minds, based on the negative traumatic experiences we have faced in our pasts.

Once you figure out the difference, then you can teach yourself to distrust the stories your mind tries to create for you.

- **Heal your heart**

It is best to give yourself, and your heart, extra time to heal. Give yourself patience and self-love. This may be extra difficult for some people, but reaching out for help through a professional is not as scary as it seems. Understand that not everyone is out to get you and betray you, but it will take some time before trusting this thought. As we get lost along our journey, we need to keep in mind that trust is something we will achieve with great effort and hard work. If you want to trust, you must be dedicated to putting the pieces back together.

Dealing With Self-Doubt. Trust Yourself

Our freedom is limited by feelings of self-doubt and is replaced by fear and anxiety. We must learn how to deal with this and trust ourselves to be able to open our shell and live comfortably in our own skin. Once we learn how to trust ourselves, we can further progress to trusting others based on our newly learned self-awareness and confidence. These tips are to help you gain confidence, start listening to yourself, and trust that what you believe is acceptable by nature.

- **Restore your inner self**

The most important step to getting rid of self-doubt and opening the door to freedom is by finding out how to love yourself. Let go of the beliefs the world or other people have brainwashed you to believe, and start your journey for truth and self-understanding. You can learn this skill through meditation, learning about self-awareness, spending time alone with your thoughts, finding your inner voice and making friends - not enemies - with yourself.

Once you find peace and balance, you learn how to let go of the small things and cope with the bigger things. Self-doubt comes from what we have learned from the world around us. We are brainwashed by magazines, TV, music, and entertainment through technology. If you are constantly comparing yourself to what the world wants you to become, then you are living in a world trying to please others. When you learn to let this go, it won't matter what you surround yourself with, because you will come to trust your instincts, hence trusting yourself will come easily.

- **Accept your faults**

Comprehend that nobody is flawless - not even you. When you stop trying to please everyone and perfect everything you do, you learn that being who you are, as you are, is perfectly imperfect. When you accept that the experiences you have gone through shapes you into who you are today, you become one with yourself and the rest of the world will follow.

All of your strengths and weaknesses make up who you are. There is nothing you can do about it most times and, if there is, then work at it. Remember to reward yourself, and take care of yourself because rewarding yourself sets you up for having a happy soul. A happy soul makes for a happy person. A happy person makes for a happy life. See where I am going with this?

- **Appreciate failure**

The world that we live in has tried to convince us that failure is bad. When we see the word failure or feel failure within ourselves, we tend to associate it with bad, negative feelings. In fact, this is wrong in all aspects. If we didn't fail, then we would never learn. If we never committed errors, we could never develop.

So fail, and fail again. Make as many mistakes as you can and convince yourself that it is okay. Tell yourself you can and will succeed, but not without a few hiccups along the way. When you fall down, get right back up again because the truth of the matter is, is that you cannot succeed without first failing.

- **Be accountable for your life**

There are often times when we are too quick to judge someone else for our decisions or feelings. We put the blame of our actions on others' shoulders as a way to make do with the mistakes we have made. By blaming someone else, we don't own up to how we feel. Do you ever catch yourself saying "You are making me feel this way," or "Because of you, I had to do this?" It is because you feel you are not in control of your own life, so passing the blame to someone else is just easier.

When you take responsibility for your own actions, choices, thoughts, beliefs, and stop feeling victimized by everything and everyone around you, you will notice yourself becoming freer. You will feel the weight lift off your shoulders to gain insight into who you need to be. Confidence, courage, and self-trust will come from you taking the initiative that you are the only person who controls your life and everything that goes on in it.

Overcome Fear to Trust Yourself Again

There are different areas in trusting ourselves. When we struggle in one thing, we excel in the next, that's just life. Trusting that we will fail, however, is like setting ourselves up to struggle more. The media shows us quotes on topics, such as how to prove the haters wrong, showing your boss who is the boss, or who wears the pants in your relationship, and how to make someone jealous. Although these motivations can be funny, sometimes inspiring and make sense the way they are written, they will not set you up for success but instead, give you temporary accomplishments.

The ultimate question is: What does trusting yourself feel and look like?

Trusting yourself takes on many roles and involves deep layers of self-evaluation and acceptance. Here are a few pointers on where to start:

- **Know that you can handle any outcome**

When you trust yourself, it means that you believe enough in yourself that you can and will succeed. Only when we do not succeed and we expect too much of ourselves is when it will lead to having trust issues within ourselves. The thing to keep in mind here is that you will survive no matter the outcome. Believing in yourself that you can handle negative emotions, such as failure and rejection, is the key to learning how to manage your trust issues within yourself.

- **Believe in yourself that you know better**

Throughout our lives based on our experiences, we develop negative thoughts that we are not consciously aware of. We all can uncover these irrational, self-defeating messages if we listen to ourselves and learn to trust that we know better. When you learn to relax and let go of what will happen, or not happen, and listen to your true instincts, is when you will find peace and strength to trust yourself.

- **Quit persuading yourself through discipline**

The minute you stop believing in yourself is the minute you set yourself up for failure, and then the continued beliefs that you are not worthy is when it becomes impossible to trust yourself. It is all based on the state of mind (as I mentioned previously). When you tell yourself "I can, I believe, and I will," you train your brain to trust yourself knowing that you have the strength to do so. If you are one of those people second-guessing your strengths and always looking for reassurance, then you do not trust yourself and you are toxic to yourself.

- **Value yourself, and everything you have done to get to where you are now**

As mentioned before, the failures you make in life are to set you up for success, so it is good to fail, meaning it will only teach you lessons that are crucial to look back on. Whether you have been stuck in the same cycle, constantly coming back to what has been previously done, or you are taking steps forward just to take a couple back, the fact is, is that you should look at all of this as accomplishments.

When you trust yourself, reflecting on what you have accomplished or have failed to achieve is all aligned to help you become who you are today. Trust that who you are is good and pure based on your own popular beliefs. No-one can convince you that you are not good enough if you believe that you are, and that is the only thing that matters.

Fixing the problem of trust issues starts and ends with you. You are the only master in this journey called life. No-one else can live your life for you or tell you how to live it. Not trusting yourself and your beliefs are the only things standing in your way of having a fulfilled life. Change has to be your first step, and taking a moment to address these internal thoughts is key to becoming better at growing into who you want to become.

Chapter Six
Building Trust

"Only trust someone who can see these three things in you: the sorrow behind your smile, the love behind your anger, and the reason behind your silence" - Unknown

If you have made it this far in the steps to overcoming trust issues within yourself and your environment, then congratulations to getting to the last chapter. This chapter explains the last step to recovery after you manage to trust yourself and new people around you. Here is where you can start letting people build your trust back, where you can start building more trust within yourself, and you can also learn how to build trust with other people you may have wronged.

By this point, if you still don't trust yourself, the first step is to learn how to build it before you can fix it. Everybody's minds are different in the way we process and learn so, whatever way works for you, works for you. Be okay with this process.

The benefits of trusting yourself is a lot more rewarding to the disadvantages to not trusting yourself as explained in this book.

How to Build Trust in Yourself

Building trust in yourself can help with your decision-making skills and boost your self-confidence levels. If you constantly fear you are making the wrong choice and searching for reassurance, then this says that you still don't trust yourself resulting in the loss of many great opportunities.

Stop criticizing yourself and start believing that you know the answers.

- **Be yourself**

Other people will be able to sense when you are self-conscious and have low self-esteem. This makes it easier for them to take advantage of you, and use your weaknesses against you; thus, resulting in more lack of trust for yourself ending in a vicious cycle that is hard to get out of.

When you start to feel self-doubt or insecurities in front of people, just tell yourself that it's okay to be you, and there is nothing wrong with who you are. Practice around people you know, so it becomes easier when you are around strangers and new people. When practicing, take note of how you're feeling and where you start to feel the most uncomfortable. Repeat this process until you feel better and less insecure around the people you love. Test your strengths by bringing up topics that you would have previously been upset about. This is called exposure therapy.

Once people feel they can trust you and not take advantage of you, you will be able to have more confidence in yourself to trust yourself again.

- **Set logical goals**

If we set expectations too high and don't complete the tasks we have set for ourselves in the time or manner that we have decided, we often fail. With failure comes judgment, and trusting ourselves with the next project will be judged by second-guessing and under-estimating our ability to achieve that goal.

Again, failure is not a bad thing, but do not purposely set yourself up for failure. Once you fail, accept that it was a lesson and a mistake that you will try not to repeat again. Accept it, acknowledge it, and move on.

- **Be kind and patient with yourself**

We all have souls that need to be replenished. We all have that inside voice that tries to make decisions for ourselves. Whether we trust that voice or we go against it is due to our better judgment based on what we know and what we have been through. Looking after yourself is fundamental for a healthy brain to be able to trust yourself. We all fall down, but it doesn't mean we can't get back up again. Keep this thought rolling and problems won't seem as big.

By taking care of yourself and your own needs first, it means you have love for yourself and make sure you are okay first. This is not to be selfish or to come off as better than anyone else. Example: If you can't take care of yourself and love yourself, then you will not be able to take care of and love someone else to the best of your ability.

So, how do you do this? Listen to your thoughts – the voice inside your head that makes discussions with you. What is the tone? Is it cruel, or is it nice? Judging or accepting? When you learn to love yourself, confidence will strike within you and will radiate to other people, resulting in trust for yourself, and others will see that they can trust you as well.

- **Progress from your strengths**

When you are good or great at something, build the trust that you are great at it and pay attention to the feeling you get once successful with these strengths. Take a mental note of the emotions you feel when you succeed. This can happen also with your weaknesses. When you make a mistake, go back to the feeling you felt when you achieved it, and draw from that energy while keeping a healthy thought process that a mistake doesn't mean you failed.

Be great at what you are good at, and do the best you can at what you are not so good at. Understand that you are not perfect and you are not superman or superwoman. If you continue to do the best you can in any situation that you are faced with, then at least if it doesn't work out, you can walk away knowing and trusting yourself that you did what you could. Move on and don't dwell on this.

- **Be alone**

Don't be alone with yourself constantly, and I don't mean that you isolate yourself. I mean to spend some time with yourself to get to know more about who you are and who you want to be. Spending time alone with your thoughts can really help you pinpoint where your trust issues come from, and with this, you can make steps towards fixing the problem. If you are a person that is not good at being alone with yourself, try meditation and reflection on your doubts. Ask yourself why it is so bad to do this for yourself. You must break the habit of trying to distract yourself and just be patient with your thoughts.

When you can finally rest and look within yourself, notice your thoughts and let them go. Do not judge them or label them as good thoughts or bad thoughts. Notice them, asses them, pay attention to the tone of them and move on. When we stop giving our negative thoughts or positive thoughts attention, we learn to address hard situations and make better decisions on how to fix problems.

- **Be decisive**

When you make a decision, stick to it. Don't look back, don't look forward. Focus on the moment and the present. There are often times when we are faced with a complication and we think too much about it. When we think too much about something, it gives us time to second-guess or question whether or not we are doing the right thing. Trust yourself that the first or second answer you have is the right one and stick with it.

The only thing you should reflect on is learning from the mistakes and failures you made last time. If this still turns out to be the wrong choice, don't sit and dwell and beat yourself up about it. Just know that next time you will do better and make the right one. Think about the success that can happen from making this decision and go with it. If you succeed, the next time you have to decide on something, you will trust that you know what to do. Always make sure you are not focusing on the 'what ifs.' Too many times we are faced with and questioned with the 'what ifs.' Imagine if there was no 'what if' scenario. What you can't change now is not worth dwelling on and stressing about as it is only hurting you and setting you up for more complications. When the 'what if' happens, deal with it at the moment it happens. Here is a thought - what if there was no 'what ifs?'

In conclusion, trusting yourself is the most rewarding thing you can do to set yourself up for a brighter future. A world of self-doubt and low self-esteem only hurts you and the people around you. Creating a better environment for you is the best thing you can do for yourself.

Ways to Rebuild Trust in Your Relationships

'A relationship without trust is like a car without gas – it is not going to go anywhere' is a very common saying. This means that, to have a healthy relationship, you must have trust for each other.

When we have lied to our spouse or partner in the past, a whole world of trust issues come into play and it becomes almost impossible to rebuild. With great effort on both parts, the trust will come in due time. The reason honesty is important in a relationship is that it allows us to live in reality instead of a fantasy where made-up beliefs are being accused due to the deceitful action.

So, let's talk about ways to rebuild that connection between you two so you can get back on track.

- **Know yourself and your intent**

When we know who we truly are, it will become easier for us to be honest with ourselves and someone else. When we don't trust ourselves, we are conforming to what the world tells us to do (as explained earlier) meaning we fill our brains with a series of 'shoulds' or 'should haves.'

It is important to understand where your thoughts come from so, if they tell you no, stop or run, find some truth behind why you may be thinking this way. Differentiate between harmful influences and what we want. Once we know where our thoughts are coming from, we can then make actions or decisions based on how much truth or proof you have behind the thoughts.

When we learn how to do this, we can be honest with ourselves and the people that we love because we know what we want, and what the outcome we want to achieve is. If you find yourself blaming the other person, or telling them what they want to hear, thus resulting in shame, go back and figure out why and where your thoughts are coming from.

- **Say what you mean, and mean what you say**

When we become comfortable, familiar, and we think the other person will stay with us no matter what, we are setting ourselves up for false hope. The truth is that you are always at risk of losing the relationship. Sometimes, people get so comfortable with the other person that they stop trying to keep them. If this happens, sparks are lost, feelings become distant, and we start to pull away subconsciously.

A 'fantasy bond' is an illusion of connection that replaces loving ways to relate to the other person. When this happens, it is due to your love life becoming a matter of routine rather than adventure. If you constantly fight or argue, the spark you had in the beginning, it becomes lost and, eventually, you struggle to find why you continue to stay in the relationship. This can all happen from a lack of trust.

To avoid this happening, make sure you never stop trying to act with integrity and matching what you're saying through your actions. Example: If you say you are in love, or that you love that person, then do things that will convince the other person that you do love them. Making the other person happy should never become a difficult task. The book *"The Five Love Languages: The Secret to a Love that Lasts"* by Gary Chapman is a great book to read, teaching you how to make the other person happy through quality time, words of affirmation, receiving gifts, acts of service, and physical touch. It explains the love meter and how much or less you are giving your partner. When the love meter is full, there is less time for complications.

Moving on: It is important to show how we feel, and engage with each other on a more intimate level through body language. Of course, with trust issues at hand, it is most difficult to express this to your partner. Ask yourself why you may have lied before or maybe why they have lied to you. When you say "I love you," do you look into their eyes and speak to them with kindness, or do you sigh and roll your eyes as to address anger and hostility towards them? One of the biggest reasons our partners have lied to us or hid something is that they are not fully satisfied with your behavior, so open up, and let them in.

- **Be sincere in your actions**

When in a healthy relationship, not everything is easy to talk about and, regardless, there are fights or arguments. It is important to remember not to address the same fight over and over again as this can be tiring on both of you. We can be blunt and straight to the point, all while having a calm and reluctant tone. This doesn't mean you are being cruel or hurtful. When you say you will let something go, and you turn around and you're arguing about the same thing in your next fight, there will be a new form of trust issues within the relationship in which you are trying to rebuild or vice versa.

When we get close to someone that will let us get close enough to them, they are trusting you with their flaws, negative tendencies, and defense actions. They trust you to accept them this way and expect the same from you. When you are not open with your partner about what you feel and observe, or when difficulties with communication gets in the way, you may grow cynical and build cases against them that will exaggerate their flaws and make matters worse - not better.

Instead of creating a world of hostility and automatically attacking or questioning, try to be more sincere and vulnerable. When you say or feel "You are always working, it feels like we have no time together, so I guess that's just how it is," turn it into something more positive and less attacking like "I miss spending time together, but you work all the time." This shows that you understand they have to work, but you are expressing how you feel which is missing them. In return, they may cut down their hours or take more days off depending on what they do. When your partner reacts to you in a hostile way, try to keep your composure by saying "I feel threatened or less attracted to you when you try to control what we do together or act tough towards me." This opens the door for a healthy discussion about the way you feel rather than criticizing them and their every move. Try to use 'I feel' statements, rather than 'you' statements.

When we address our partner this way, regardless of how uncomfortable it makes them or you feel, it comes from a place of vulnerability and openness, which can lead to closeness and intimacy. You may fight and argue, but as long as both parties are trying to be less judgmental and more honest, the relationship will become less toxic and more healthy.

- **Be open to their thoughts**

We can't expect to say our peace and then shut them out when they speak. Remember to listen to understand, do not listen to respond. This includes behaviors such as not interrupting them, giving them enough time to express what they are trying to say, and giving them enough space to show your body language is not to be hostile, but to be gentle. If your partner says to you they feel you are hot-headed and temperamental when you do such things, don't judge them, but be mindful of the honesty they are giving you. This is hard for them too and it is not all about you as you are not the only one having, and experiencing these problems.

When our partner tries to tell us what they are feeling from the inside, make sure you are looking for the core truth and problem behind their words rather than arguing about every small detail. When it is your turn to speak, make sure you have collected your thoughts throughout the conversation they are trying to speak with you about and don't react with defensive, reactive, or punishing feedback. When we feel threatened by criticism, we tend to emotionally manipulate our partner which leads to nowhere and it will get the relationship nowhere. When we become hostile in our feedback, it sets up our partners to react.

Being deceitful is not always what your partner wants to do, but as mentioned earlier, when our partner feels unloved or unappreciated, they act out of nature which is to run or to shut down. It is best to try not to do this if we really want to make things work. We want a partner who feels comfortable enough to come to us for anything. We want them to be honest and to grow with us. Everything you want, I can guarantee he/she wants.

- **Accept your partner as their own individual**

Understand that they are not and will not think the same as you. You have to realize that they had a life before they met you, and you cannot control or begin to understand that world. All you need to focus on is the here and now with them by your side, so when your partner doesn't see your side or see things the way you do, it does not, by any manner, mean that they are lying. It only means that you are two separate people observing the world from different perspectives. Understand that you will not agree on everything hence what may cause fights. Fighting your point without understanding their point only leads to more serious problems in which a counselor will need to be involved. Accept your partner for they are, not for who you want them to be. Accept the way they think and not for how you want them to think and act. When you come to this realization, you will come to a road that leads to a healthier relationship.

Rebuilding trust consists of the willingness to be truthful when it's uncomfortable and it is always the give and take throughout the partnership. The bottom line is if you love each other and want to make things work then conclude that you are two individuals who choose to be together despite your differences. To love someone is to love their flaws and imperfections too. When two people **choose** to be together, then it stems from choice rather than being in a fantasy that you feel trapped in.

Make the choice to stay, or make the choice to leave, but make sure it's the choice you want for you, not for anyone else.

Conclusion

This eBook was intended to help you or whoever reads it to learn about trust and trust issues. I have researched many resources and have made sure that all the information in this book is up to date and professional. When people think about trust issues, they become quick to judge on if the people around them have trust issues. This book was written to inform you, as the reader that you may also, have trust issues.

To fully understand the concept of this book, I hope you read it with an open mind and engage with the information provided. Did you learn something? Do you have any more questions after reading it? Maybe this was information you already knew. My hope is that whatever your situation or intake on this eBook is, you have at least come to a conclusion that trust issues are not meant to be a bad thing and can be fixed with the right state of mind.

Bonus Material: Earning – An Introduction To Earning With The Double Your Income Sequence

SECTION 1: THE SECRET OF FORMING MONEY HABITS (AND HOW TO ENFORCE THEM)

You are a collection of your favorite habits.

And, you have a niche set of habits that contribute to the money you can earn and keep, during your average month. Understanding the science behind these habits will help you positively influence the energy you spend on making more money.

A habit is a practice that you have used so often, that it has become an internalized, autonomic blueprint – a kind of default program for how to execute a specific action.[1]

Habits become damaging when they stop being beneficial, and instead, become uncontrollable, unintentional and contrary to your personal goals. Most individuals carry with them the burden of many bad habits, which inadvertently keeps them from forging ahead and achieving their income goals.

According to Charles Duhigg, the reason why we struggle with habits is that they are as unique as we are. There is no quick-fix formula.

---

[1] Habit, Wikipedia, https://en.wikipedia.org/wiki/Habit

In order to effectively change your habits, you need enlightenment on a better process, and, on your stuck behavior. Then you can change your *cue-routine-reward* cycle.[2]

Cue: a trigger that puts your brain in automatic mode and chooses your habit

Routine: A physical, mental or emotional set of actions

Reward: What you gain from executing the habit

With fresh ideas and an understanding of how to break bad habit loops, you will adopt powerful new habits that will help you double your income every, single, month.

SECTION 2: HOW TO CREATE NEW MONEY HABITS

New habits are how you will double your income.

This means you need to:

#1: Identify and break bad habits, to free up room for fresh practices

#2: Identity and consciously adopt new habits, until they become automatic

This guide is not about the first step. If you want to learn how to break bad habits, I suggest reading Charles Duhigg's classic, "The Power of Habit."

---

[2] Duhigg, Charles, How Habits Work, https://charlesduhigg.com/how-habits-work/

What you do need to realize, is that a number of your existing habits need to change, to make room for the ones outlined in this guide. You must become consciously aware of your *cue-routine-reward cycle*, and interrupt it to stay on track.

You can do this effectively by replacing your existing rewards, with your new goal to double your income. To create a new habit, follow this simple process.

- **Identify the bad habit that must be replaced**

    ➢ Waking up at 7 am to be at work at 8 am

- **Identify the harm it's causing**

    ➢ Rushing and feeling harassed and irritated when you get to work

- **Understand and replace the reward from your bad habit**

    ➢ Instead of instant gratification from sleeping late, your mood will be elevated, and your energy levels will be high at work

- **Implement the new habit, motivated by a stronger overall reward**

    ➢ Practice waking up at 5 am, arriving at work at 7:30 and easing into your day, to stimulate the positive mindset required for success

According to modern studies, it takes roughly 66 days before a new behavior becomes automatic.[3]

SECTION 3: THE 14 HABITS THAT WILL DOUBLE YOUR INCOME

Here are the habits you need.

Habit 1: SLEEP (You're Not Doing It Right)

Bill Gates, the co-founder of Microsoft, sleeps for 7 hours every night and reads for 1 hour before bedtime.

With over a third of Americans not getting enough regular sleep, most people vastly underestimate the importance of quality shuteye in their lives.

Over or under-sleeping exposes you to increased risk for chronic conditions, mental distress, stroke and heart disease.[4] According to a 2018 Poll by The National Sleep Foundation, excellent sleepers feel more effective at getting things done the next day.[5]

The first habit you need to adopt is simple – get high quality, regular sleep.

Set a time every evening to go to sleep and stick to it. You should be in bed an hour before, your phone off and all screens far away from you. Read for an hour. Then, go to sleep for 7.

---

[3] Lally, Phillippa, How are Habits Formed: Modelling Habit Formation in the Real World, https://onlinelibrary.wiley.com/doi/abs/10.1002/ejsp.674

[4] 1 in 3 Adults Don't Get Enough Sleep, https://www.cdc.gov/media/releases/2016/p0215-enough-sleep.html

[5] National Sleep Foundation's 2018 Sleep in America Poll Shows Americans Failing to Prioritize Sleep, https://sleepfoundation.org/media-center/press-release/2018-sleep-in-america-poll-shows

Wake up promptly, 7 hours later. Not a minute more.

Sticking to this new habit promises you stronger immunity, the improved concentration at work and greater emotional stability overall. Consistency will ensure that your circadian rhythms function well, and you never have trouble with restless sleep or with falling asleep.[6]

✓	Adopt this positive sleep habit

Habit 2: EXERCISE (It's Not Enough, or It's Too Much)

Ex-President Barack Obama works out for 45 minutes a day, six days a week. Thirty minutes or more of aerobic exercise is done daily by 76% of all successful people.[7]

Aerobic exercise is the one consistent habit that will give you the energy you need to succeed. You should run, walk, jog, bike or take a class at the gym. Cardio gets your blood pumping, which is ideal for your brain and boosts your intelligence.[8]

The second habit you need to adopt – find and practice an aerobic exercise, daily.

---

[6] Mahabir, Nicole, How and Why Waking Up at the Same Time Every Day Can Improve Your Health, https://www.cbc.ca/life/wellness/how-and-why-waking-up-at-the-same-time-everyday-can-improve-your-health-1.4357391

[7] Cohen Jennifer, Exercise is One Thing Most Successful People Do Everyday, https://www.entrepreneur.com/article/276760

[8] Regular Exercise Releases Brain Chemicals Key for Memory, Concentration, and Mental Sharpness, From the May 2013 Harvard Men's Health Watch, https://www.health.harvard.edu/press_releases/regular-exercise-releases-brain-chemicals-key-for-memory-concentration-and-mental-sharpness

Now, you need to pick 45 minutes to an hour, every day to get your cardio in. It makes no difference whether you do this in the morning, or late in the evening – as long as it is done every single day.

Consistency is how you will reap these many benefits.

Try to pick something that fits into your life, schedule and likes. You don't have to spend money, you simply have to get active. This means finding an exercise you will enjoy. Some people like boxing classes, others prefer to take a walk around the neighborhood.

✓	Adopt this positive exercise habit

Habit 3: SOCIAL ENERGY (Here's One to Protect)

Oprah Winfrey, talk-show host, and owner of Harpo Studios meditates for 20 minutes every morning, shortly after waking up.

Meditation makes you more in-tune with yourself, how you feel, and how the world around you feels. It's great for focus, increased energy, decreased stress and lifts brain fog.[9]

The people around you have an impact on your energy levels. Successful people surround themselves with positive, go-getters – while the average person is drained by one or more toxic, or negative people in their lives. Social energy must be protected.

The third habit is – to meditate daily on how to optimize your social energy.

---

[9] Sun, Carolyn, I Tried This Oprah Meditation Hack Every Day for Two Weeks. Here Are My 5 Takeaways, https://www.entrepreneur.com/article/310039

According to a Cigna Study, loneliness is at epidemic levels in America.[10] But this is never a good reason to allow anyone a place in your life.

Take a look at your connections and consider if they add, or take energy away from you as you meditate for 20 minutes every morning.

Extroverted, or introverted, you need the right kind of connections in your daily life. If you have energy vampires in your sphere, you must get rid of them to be at your best.

✓	Adopt positive social meditation

Habit 4: SELF-INVESTMENT (Knowing and Doing)

Albert Einstein believed in constant self-investment through learning, research and application of that newfound knowledge.

The day you stop learning, is the day you stop growing. And personal growth is what takes you towards income acceleration and success. Einstein knew that constant reading was critical to learning, but so was the application of the knowledge learned while reading.

He famously said that too much reading renders the brain lazy. To grow in his field, Einstein continued to study formally until he was 26, then pursued self-study. He was not, as many believe, a naturally talented genius savant – he studied, read and practiced knowledge.[11]

---

[10] New Cigna Study Reveals Loneliness at Epidemic Levels in America, https://www.prnewswire.com/news-releases/new-cigna-study-reveals-loneliness-at-epidemic-levels-in-america-300639747.html

[11] Shead, Mark, Are You Reading Too Much?, http://www.productivity501.com/are-you-reading-too-much/8874/

The fourth habit is – invest in your field of knowledge through reading and practice.

If you want to excel like Einstein, shift from consuming entertainment to consuming knowledge. This is easily done by dedicating an hour or more to reading and applying your newly discovered knowledge. Practice what you learn, to see the real difference.[12]

Carve an hour of your day, in the morning or evening to read a book and then realize its lessons. This can be split into 30 minutes of reading, 30 minutes of creating.

✓	Learn and practice new knowledge

Habit 5: DELEGATION (Focus on The Big Picture)

Richard Branson, Founder of Virgin and hundreds of other companies, is famous for his practice of 'letting go, to grow.' He delegates to focus on the big picture.[13]

Delegation is a habit that most people fail to practice. Instead, they try to do everything themselves and end up burned out, exhausted and depleted.

When you actively practice delegation, you become a talented multitasker, able to orchestrate and design your own career. It is at this point your income will inflate.

---

[12] How Much Did Albert Einstein Study?, https://www.forbes.com/sites/quora/2017/12/28/how-much-did-albert-einstein-study/#1595adeb28bc

[13] Richard Branson: Why Delegation is Crucial for Success, https://www.virgin.com/entrepreneur/richard-branson-why-delegation-crucial-success

The fifth habit is – to practice delegation often and keep your eyes on the big picture.

Your career, or income goals, maybe the big picture for now. Knowing where you want to end up gives you clarity of purpose, and will help you assign what is not important to those around you. This must be done in all aspects of your life that consume your time.

This habit will kick in when someone makes demands on your time. Ask yourself if it contributes to your big picture. If it does not, find a creative way of delegating it to another human being. Make this a habit, and soon you will be surrounded by competent people.[14]

✓	Adopt the habit of delegation

Habit 6: MENTORING (Learning and Teaching)

Marie Forleo is a life coach, philanthropist and entrepreneur, who believes in the power of mentoring and being mentored, to become hugely successful.[15]

In fact, she uses connections to grow her business at every level. With storytelling and the ability to build a community around her lifestyle brand, she was named Oprah's *"thought leader for the next generation."*

---

[14] Coleman, Alison, Delegate Like Branson: Hire People Who are More Talented Than You, https://www.forbes.com/sites/alisoncoleman/2015/01/25/delegate-like-branson-hire-people-who-are-more-talented-than-you/#4ce10d27cb3d

[15] Brouwer, Allen, Lavery, Cathryn, Why Marie Forleo Says This One Marketing Trick Is So Important, https://www.entrepreneur.com/article/305586

Your ability to surround yourself with the right people will be the single most useful habit you can adopt. Most people never actively practice the art of conscious mentoring.

The sixth habit is – to practice attracting network connections that will help you excel!

Who do you know that could teach you something important? Have you ever met someone who you wanted to learn from? Teaching and learning is fundamental to networking, and the basis for all positive relationships, in a corporate environment.[16]

Every day, you should consciously invest more energy in stimulating and improving mentor relationships that will help you grow and succeed as a person in your field. Be ruthlessly selective about your friends and who you spend the most time with.

Allow others to mentor you, and be mentored by you, in a working environment.

✓	Adopt the habit of mentoring and being mentored

---

[16] Forleo, Marie, Networking For Introverts W/Susan Cain, https://www.marieforleo.com/2013/11/susan-cain-introverts-networking/

Habit 7: YOUR 96 MINUTES (This is Your Most Valuable Time)

Stephen King is known for his work ethic and ability to produce six good pages of writing every day consistently. He does this by following the same productivity routine daily. [17]

You need to have the discipline and consistency required, to do something for your direct productivity benefit, for 96 minutes a day. Why 96 minutes?

Science says that everyone has 96 highly productive minutes every day, a time window when you have the most energy and are at your best. If you harness this power and use it for your ultimate goal of earning more money, it shifts from possible, to probable. [18]

The seventh habit is – Spend 96 minutes a day working on your main career goal.

Discover when your 96 minutes kicks in. It might be just after waking up. It might be late at night when everyone else is sleeping. Find your window and use it.

Spend those 96 minutes focused exclusively on your main career goal. If that is to get a promotion, this is when you will plan and execute a strategy. If it is to launch a website, this is when you will put in the work.

✓	Adopt the 96-minute habit

---

[17] Cotterill, Thomas, Stephen Kings Work Habits, https://thomascotterill.wordpress.com/2012/09/13/stephen-kings-work-habits/

[18] The Rule of 96 Minutes to Productivity, http://sapience.net/blog/the-rule-of-96-minutes-to-productivity/

Habit 8: INNOVATION (Get to The Core of Things)

Elon Musk, the founder of PayPal, SpaceX and Tesla, is a known innovator and practices the Richard Feynman technique mixed with first principles, to stay creative. [19]

The underlying concept of this technique is to not try and remember, but to understand – because when you do, you automatically remember. It's a way to entertain new ideas and be creative in a way that promotes productivity.

Knowledge to Elon, is about understanding the fundamental principles of a thing,to know the trunk and branches before diving headlong into the details, or the leaves of an idea.

The eighth habit is – when learning something new, to understand its core first.

Applying this to your career will make you a forward-thinking innovator. For example, if you are a psychologist, you would benefit from learning more about neuroscience, because it is at the core of your field. Competency is all about strong, unshakable fundamentals.[20]

Spend 30 minutes every day learning something that reinforces how you innovate in your chosen field. Soon you will be questioning, brainstorming and seeing patterns that may amount to improvements you can implement.

---

[19] The Feynman Technique: The Best Way to Learn Anything, https://fs.blog/2012/04/learn-anything-faster-with-the-feynman-technique/

[20] Stillman, Jessica, 3 Smart Strategies Geniuses Like Albert Einstein and Elon Musk Use to Learn Anything Faster, http://www.businessinsider.com/3-strategies-geniuses-like-elon-musk-use-to-learn-anything-faster-2017-10?IR=T

✓	Practice innovation for 30 mins a day

Habit 9: THE WIN-WIN (Mutually Beneficial Relationships)

Stephen Covey, author of the smash hit "The 7 Habits of Highly Effective People" advocated the importance of win-win relationships.

According to Covey, most people approach life with a scarcity mindset, as opposed to an abundance mindset. Because of this, social interactions become unbalanced.[21]

There are several types of human interaction, win-lose, lose-lose, lose-win – but none are as powerful or effective as the win-win. When you practice win-win interactions, your engagements are mutually beneficial, and people will enjoy working with you.

The ninth habit is – to practice win-win human interactions in your daily life.

When you do, you will find that people flock to you, because they see the benefits of doing business with you. When everyone benefits, you can succeed together.

This habit will cue when someone asks you for something. This should be your trigger to think about how you can make the interaction a win-win scenario. Covey says, to take consideration and courage into account, and to be creative in your problem-solving.

---

[21] Hussain, Anum, 7 Habits of Highly Effective People [Book Summary], https://blog.hubspot.com/sales/habits-of-highly-effective-people-summary

As you create win-win results, your influence will grow in your field. Remember that there is enough success around for everyone, and you can create it for them!

✓	Practice win-win human interactions

Habit 10: SPEAK UP (Know and Communicate Your Value)

Tyra Banks, ex-supermodel, TV producer and personality, based her career success on the ability to speak up, negotiate and get what she desires most.

She made a habit of speaking clearly, frankly and openly about her value with the people around her. Too often, we get stuck in the habit of remaining passive, and silent about our worth. Promotions and opportunities will pass you by because you failed to speak up.

The tenth habit is – to speak up when necessary about your value as an employee.

Tyra explains, that it is a shift from an 'I need' to an 'I deserve' mindset. Instead of explaining to your employer why you need a raise, you should explain why you deserve one. This is easily done by focusing on your value – or how you positively contribute to the company.[22]

This is another habit that will cue when you identify opportunities or feel that you deserve a promotion at your job. In meetings, be open about your contributions to the success of projects or initiatives. Speak up about how you, as a person, make things better.

---

[22] Atalla, Jen, Tyra Banks on How to Ask for a Raise, http://www.businessinsider.com/tyra-banks-how-to-ask-for-a-raise-2018-4?IR=T

Getting into the habit of communicating your worth to people around you, positions you for rapid advancement. If you cannot see and communicate your value, the higher-ups will not see it either. Be persistent. Have a clear voice. And do not get lost in the crowd.

✓	Practice communicating personal value

Habit 11: PAY YOURSELF FIRST (This is Ground-breaking Advice)

George Clason was the author who wrote the classic 'The Richest Man in Babylon' and taught people to pay themselves first, in order to gain real wealth.[23]

Imagine if, since you had started working at age 21, you had put away 10% of every paycheck. This is what it means to pay yourself first. Money saved and kept earns compound interest and grows exponentially over long periods of time.

People that want to be wealthy use this strategy to move from employed earning to investing. Investing money is how you break out of your income bracket altogether.

The eleventh habit is – to put 10% of every paycheck aside to grow your wealth.

It might seem like very little at first, but 5 years of putting away just $100.00, frees up $6000.00 for investment. It gives you options to supplement your salary as you age.

---

[23] Canfield, Jack, The Key to Wealth: Pay Yourself First, http://jackcanfield.com/blog/the-key-to-wealth-pay-yourself-first/

To start the habit, every time you are paid – immediately take 10% of that total amount and put it in a separate account. You cannot touch this money. It is there simply to exist and earn you money from long-term growth.

The pay yourself first habit will help you clear away your debt, and get you investing at a young age. Get into this habit early, and you will benefit from time itself.

✓	Adopt the pay yourself first habit

Habit 12: SIDE HUSTLE (Spend Your Time for Returns)

Rob Kalin never meant Etsy.com to be such a smash success. Initially, it was simply his side hustle, born from a desire to make wood-encased computers. [24]

Rob Kalin is a furniture designer who started Etsy as a place to sell his wares. It was a side hustle, an increasingly common play among Millennials. Some 61% of Millennials work on their side hustles once a week or more.[25]

This is usually a job that earns them money beyond their 9-5, or a personal project with income potential that they are developing. What is your side hustle?

The twelfth habit is – work on your side hustle twice a week.

---

[24] Green, Penelope, Scratching an Itch, https://www.nytimes.com/2016/05/05/style/etsy-rob-kalin.html

[25] Sophy, Joshua, More Than 1 in 4 Millennials Work a Side Hustle, https://smallbiztrends.com/2017/07/millennial-side-hustle-statistics.html

On Mondays and Thursdays, or Tuesdays and Fridays you should dedicate a couple of hours to your side hustle. This is a second business, born from your creative or analytical talents that may become a solid earner for you down the line.

Scheduling in time to develop your secondary projects is important for personal growth, and increasing your income. Many Millennials discover that once their side businesses reach a certain level, they can either sell them or commit fulltime to their passions.

✓	Adopt the side hustle habit

Habit 13: SUNDAY REVIEW (3 Hours to Financial Freedom!)

Suze Orman, a personal finance expert and personality, is known for teaching people to pick just one thing about their finances to work on, at a time. [26]

She called it the 'one and done' method, and it simplifies the huge challenge of getting hold of your financial situation. Many people find their finances overwhelming, and so never take proactive steps towards understanding and controlling them.

The thirteenth habit is – to spend 3 hours every Sunday focusing on one financial problem.

You might need to save, or clear debt, or better understand your expenses and how to curb them. Whatever you need, you will tackle it during a designated time, every Sunday.

---

[26] Financial Resolutions for 2017? Just Do This One Thing, https://www.suzeorman.com/blog/financial-resolutions-for-2017-just-do-this-one-thing

When you practice the habit of reviewing your finances regularly, to better understand and control them, you will change your life.

Make sure that you pick only one simple thing at a time so that you can properly digest and institute changes as necessary. Spend the time learning and streamlining for your ultimate benefit, as a responsible financial planner.

✓	Adopt the Sunday review habit

Habit 14: MINIMALISM (Know How to Spend)

Steve Jobs, Founder of Apple, was a noted minimalist and wore the same black turtleneck every day for many, many years.

Popularized by Silicon Valley, minimalism reduces decision-fatigue, a common problem in today's overcrowded, ultra-informed society. With so much information and choice out there, it is no wonder you struggle to make good decisions for yourself.[27]

The theory goes that you can only make so many strong decisions in a day. The minimalist habit, allows you to dedicate those decisions to things that matter, like spending for value.

The fourteenth habit is – to spend with minimalism in mind.

Consumer culture is not for the truly rich. Instead, these individuals spend more money on a single item of quality, than repeated spending on numerous low-quality items.

---

[27] Steve Jobs and Minimalism, http://www.applegazette.com/ipod/steve-jobs-and-minimalism/

Get into the habit of spending money on quality items, instead of cheaper items that will wear and degrade. This will free up your time as you make fewer wardrobe decisions. Instead of spending your creative energy there, you will spend it at work, where it matters most.

Less items of higher quality will simplify and improve your life.

✓	Adopt the spending for value habit

SECTION 4: THE GOLDEN RULE OF SUCCESS SEQUENCING

Your habits determine your behavior, but one thing is more important.

Focus.

Your attention is a form of currency that will either enrich or impoverish your life. That is why they call it 'paying attention.' Focus is the literal gateway to learning, reasoning, decision-making, problem-solving and perception.[28]

That is why consistent focus on your habits is the golden rule of success.

None of the people you have read about in this guide could have succeeded without an all-encompassing focus on their daily habits. Every individual here keeps a rigorous, personalized schedule that optimizes these habits.

---

[28] Dr Taylor, Jim, Focus is The Gateway to Business Success, https://www.huffingtonpost.com/dr-jim-taylor/focus-is-the-gateway-to-b_b_4206552.html

Success, like your daily habits, is incredibly personal. Only you can decide when you have achieved a high enough level of success. And your habits are the stepping stones!

If you want to double your income, nothing is keeping you from it, but your habits. When you remove the bad and replace it with these powerful income-generating habits, you will immediately experience rapid change that will reshape your life.

That is why your primary focus must be a habitual practice, according to a personalized schedule. Without it, expect to fall back into bad patterns of behavior.

SECTION 5: THESE HABITS WILL MATTER MOST!

According to a study from Northwestern University, a domino effect happens when you adopt one lasting good habit.[29]

In other words, exercising every day will encourage positive eating habits. In turn, this may spread to you getting better quality sleep and performing better at work. Management of these small, seemingly insignificant habits starts with internalizing just one.

I want you to pick a habit from this list to act as your linchpin habit.

Then I want you to dedicate the next 66 days to internalizing that habit, and when you feel capable, adopt more from this list.

---

[29] Clear, James, How to Create a Chain Reaction of Good Habits, https://jamesclear.com/domino-effect

Even if you struggle to adopt more of these habits, I want you to commit to just the one. At no point over the next 66 days will you, at any point, stop practicing that habit.

The first couple in this list have the most impact. They directly affect your daily performance. This is how you will naturally double your income in the short term.

Consider the domino effect active in you right now. But it is focused on negative habits. Switch to replacing them with positive habits, and you will soar!

The habits that matter most are the ones you learn to keep. Make them part of who you are, and soon you will leap an income bracket.

SECTION 6: WILLPOWER OR WONTPOWER: YOU DECIDE

The number 1 barrier to change is a mysterious thing called 'willpower.'

Those who have it are strong. Those who lack willpower are weak.

That is what we are taught to believe in our modern society. Your ability to resist short-term temptations is chalked up to your measure of willpower.

But you are never told what it is, or how to get it. How is it meant to take over, when you have no idea how it works?

Now I am going to lift the veil.

Willpower is little more than self-control. It is the conscious act of choosing what is right, over what is easy. It is picking cognition, over emotion. It is discipline.[30]

Willpower is a *habit*.

Right now, you habitually give in to your desires. What you need to do is replace this with your long-term plan for success. Say no to instant gratification!

Practice consciously choosing to focus on what is most important, every day.

If you don't want to exercise, use your willpower. Emotions drive your thoughts. Replace them with conscious thoughts that are more beneficial. You must exercise, to feel good today, tomorrow, this week. You must exercise to earn more and be better.

Practice willpower as a habit, and soon it will take over.

SECTION 7: REGAINING YOUR FAITH IN FREE WILL

'But I have so much to do.'

'I'll begin after my major project is over.'

'I'll just let this week pass, and I'll be ready.'

It is human nature to wait for the ideal time to change. You might have bought this guide with the intent to adopt these habits 'at some point.'

---

[30] What You Need to Know About Willpower: The Psychological Science of Self-Control, http://www.apa.org/helpcenter/willpower.aspx

This is because you have lost faith in free will. Free will is your ability to choose between different courses of action, unimpeded. Now, life is all about impediments, but that does not mean you cannot choose to be better. You can.

We are all made up of a unique blend of strengths, weaknesses, circumstances and perceptions. Your free will must be exercised in accordance with your make-up, within your unique context, under your special circumstances.

The price of freedom is struggling.

The price of earning more is learning to be better.[31]

Then being better – every day!

If you cannot be better consistently, hope is lost.

In this way, free will gives you the opportunity to be whoever you want, as long as you are willing to go through the wringer to get there. It will be hard! If it were easy, everyone would be successful and living these rare lives.

My advice to be something is to practice.

Start and start *today*.

---

[31] Dr Schwartz, Seth, Do We Have Free Will, https://www.psychologytoday.com/us/blog/proceed-your-own-risk/201311/do-we-have-free-will

Check Out Our Other Books:

1. *Resolving Anxiety and Panic Attacks*

A Guide to Overcoming Severe Anxiety, Controlling Panic Attacks and Reclaiming Your Life Again

Worldwide, one in six people is affected by a mental health disorder. So you are not alone in this (Ritchie & Roser, 2019). There is a difference between clinical anxiety and everyday anxiety. Everyday anxiety is normal and in often cases, it is necessary, while chronic anxiety will leave you functionally impaired. This book will not only inform you about anxiety and panic attacks but also introduce you to various methods and techniques that aid in getting rid of anxiety. It is a perfect package if you want to make long-lasting, meaningful changes in your life in a way that gets rid of anxiety. Knowledge is power, so gaining information about anxiety and panic attacks already puts you in the lead against them.

In the first chapter, we'll start with the basic knowledge of panic attacks and anxiety. The symptoms of both are pretty much the same, but there are some major differences as well. Knowing their difference and similarities can help you clearly understand your condition. Some basic ways of coping with them are also explained alongside their symptoms.

After gaining knowledge about anxiety and panic attacks in the first section, you will seek answers and ways to overcome them. The second chapter goes more in detail about the physical effects of anxiety. There are some types of anxiety which are also talked briefly about in the chapter. There are also therapies and treatments that are used to overcome and control anxiety. Their details are discussed in the chapter from where you can figure out what sort of treatment will suit you better. Some other ways of coping with anxiety are also discussed and they will surely prove beneficial to the reader.

The third chapter will make you aware of how interrelated physical and mental healths are. There are also details on how to improve one's physical health to influence a person's anxiety positively. You will also learn how important practicing well-being is. If you are to ignore physical health, it will cause problems for your mental health as well.

The fourth chapter will delve deep into mindfulness and its vast benefits. Mindfulness is a very powerful tool we have but don't know how to use. It can be practiced through meditation techniques, etc. It makes us see things more clearly than ever before. Practicing Mindfulness will arm you against any anxiety and panic attacks. In this chapter, it is explained in detail what it means and what are its advantages.

In the fifth chapter, we will learn about meditation and how can it help manage anxiety. We first start off by knowing what it is. You also have got to know its benefits and various techniques from which one can pick according to their choice. We will also learn the accurate posture you should have during meditation. We will learn how mediation reinforces our brain to stave off anxiety and panic attacks. It is a long road but a successful one for sure. Besides helping us out with anxiety and panic disorder, meditation has numerous other benefits for our body and mind.

The sixth chapter will explore the meaning behind self-love and its importance in fighting anxiety. Our battle with anxiety has to start from a positive ground. We first have to be fully comfortable and respectful towards ourselves. You will also find out how lack of self-love can actually breed anxiety.

Opening about anxiety is not an easy task but could be very helpful against anxiety. How to go about the whole process is talked about in detail in the seventh chapter. You will also learn how to evaluate your therapist and choose the right one. In this chapter, there are also guidelines for people who have just recently become aware of their anxiety and now they want to seek help. It will give them knowledge about things to consider when talking to someone about mental health, what you should accept and be prepared for. There is also information about talk therapy there.

In the eighth chapter, we address the misunderstanding about anxiety. Despite affecting so many people, it remains a different experience for all of them. There are also common mistakes pointed out in that chapter which we'll go into detail the mistakes that make our anxiety worse.

The ninth chapter is about where we talk about putting our foot down and start to incorporate practices into our life which will help you get rid of anxiety and panic attacks. We will learn how to manage our responses. It is basically a comprehensive listing of all the things you should be avoiding or adapting to lead a healthy lifestyle free of anxiety.

Want to read more? Purchase our book on **Anxiety and Panic Attacks** *today!*

2. *Cognitive Behavioral Therapy*

How CBT Can Be Used to Rewire Your Brain, Stop Anxiety, and Overcome Depression

Cognitive stems from cognition, which encapsulates the idea of how we learn and the knowledge that we carry. The things you learn are part of your cognition, and what you do with that information is included in that category as well. Cognition includes a wide list of information that you might not fully realize.

Behavior is what we do. It is how we act. The things that you choose to say to other people are all about your behavior. How you react to what others have to say will exhibit your behavior as well. Your behavior is all about your mind interacting with your body and how that interacts with the people and other things that surround you.

Therapy is any form of help, usually from a trained professional, to help improve on whatever the therapy is specified for. You might get physical therapy to help regain strength in your knee after having a serious surgery. You can also get therapy to help overcome an alcohol or drug addiction.

Throughout this book, we're going to give you the basis you need to start understanding cognitive behavioral therapy. The three together—cognitive, behavioral, therapy—all make up CBT, which is a method that is going to directly help you overcome the mental illness that you are hoping to treat.

Therapy can be expensive, and even if you do have the means to go through with this process, you might struggle to find the right therapist. Sometimes, you might live in an area where there is only one therapist within a close distance, but you don't have a vibe with them that you find to be helpful. You might also find that you are desperate for help and that you want a therapist, but insurance coverage isn't always good for this.

By reading this book, you'll be able to find the tools you need to help with overcoming your most challenging thoughts. We are going to take you through the steps to identify the root issues and come up with specific methods to get you through.

Want to read more? Purchase our book on **Cognitive Behavioral Therapy** *today!*

3. *Effective Guide On How to Sleep Well Everyday*

The Easy Method For Better Sleep, Insomnia And Chronic Sleep Problems

"A well spent day brings happy sleep." — *Leonardo da Vinci*

Are you experiencing the worst restless feeling? Has your doctor diagnosed you with insomnia, restlessness, sleeplessness? When the whole world around you seems to be in peaceful deep slumber, you are the one who is restless. No matter what term is used to describe it, the fact is that it is you who is actually going through insomnia, and nothing could feel worse than that.

So you drag yourself from bed in the morning feeling as earth, with its entire lock stock and barrel, has decided to perch on your head for the day. Yet you go through the motions of the day, though you barely manage to make it through the hours. By the early night, you fall on to bed hoping this night will be different because you're dead tired and nothing will keep you from sleeping like a log. It's 2.00 a.m. now, dawn is breaking through and there you are, still wide awake and ready to scream to the world because no matter how tired you are or how hard you have tried, you simply can't get to sleep.

While there are proven facts and evidence of the devastating effects of sleeping less, the investigations are still on to establish the exact nature of effects resulting from too much sleep. Some researchers argue that people who sleep much longer than necessarily have a higher death rate. Physical and mental conditions such as depression or socioeconomic status can also lead to excessive sleep. There are other researchers who argue that the human body will naturally restrain it from sleeping more hours than really necessary. However, with research still underway for concrete evidence of the effects of over sleeping the best path you can choose is to adopt a sleeping pattern somewhere in the middle. According to the National Sleep Foundation, this middle range falls between seven and eight hours of sleep during the night. Despite these statistics, the best way to ensure you receive sufficient sleeping time is to let your own body act as your guide. You can always sleep a little extra if you feel exhausted or sleep a little less than usual if you feel you are oversleeping.

Dangers of Sleep deprivation.

Though sleep is something the average human being takes for granted, it is also one of the greatest mysteries in life. Just like we still don't have all the answers to the quantum field or gravity, researchers are still exploring the reasons behind the 'whats' and 'whys' of sleep. However, one fact unchallenged about sleep is that a proper sleep is paramount for maintaining good health. The general guideline regarding the optimal amount of sleep for an adult range from six to eight hours! If you carry on with too little or too much of this general guideline you are exposing yourself to the risk of adverse health effects.

Though sleep is something that comes naturally to many people, the problems of sleep deprivation have today become a pressing problem with more and more people succumbing to chronic sleeping disorders. Unfortunately, a great number of these people do not even realize that lack of sleep or sleep deprivation is at the root of their manifold problems in life. Scientific research also points out that lack of sleep on a continuous scale can lead to severe repercussions on your health.

If you have been experiencing impaired sleep patterns for a longer period, you also face the risk of:

- Severely impairing your immunity strength

- Promoting the risk of tumor growth, as it has been scientifically established that a tumor can grow at least two to three times faster among animals subjected to severe sleeping dysfunctions within a laboratory setting.

- Creating a pre-diabetic condition in the body. Insomnia creates hunger, making you want to eat even when you have already had a meal. This situation can lead to problems of obesity in turn.

- Critically impairing memory. How many times during the day have you found it difficult to remember even the most mundane and repetitive events when you have had no more than 4 – 5 hours of sleep? Even a single night of impaired sleep plays havoc with our memory faculties, just think what it can do to your brain if you consistently lose sleep.

- Ruining your performance level both physically and mentally as your problem-solving abilities will not be working in peak order.

- Stomach ulcers

- Constipation, hemorrhoids

- Heart diseases

- Depression, lethargy and other mood disorders

- Daytime drowsiness

- Irritability

- Low energy

- Low mental clarity

- Reaction time slows down

- Lower productivity

- More accidents and mistakes

- Lower levels of growth hormone and testosterone

The growth hormone in the body which is vital for maintaining our looks, energy, and skin texture is produced by the pituitary gland. The specialty of this hormone production procedure is that it is only produced during the times of deep slumber or during intense workout sessions. In the absence of normal production of the growth hormone, our bodies will start on a premature aging process. According to research, people suffering from chronic insomnia are three times more susceptible to contract fatal diseases. When you lose sleep overnight, you cannot make up for it by sleeping more the next day. A night's lost sleep will be lost forever. More alarmingly if you continue to lose sleep regularly, they will create a cumulative negative effect that will disrupt your general health. All in all, sleeping deficiencies can effectively make your life miserable, as you already know.

How Much Sleep Do I Really Need?

This is a question that remains a mystery just like the questions of why and what makes us want to sleep. In response to a question of how many hours of sleep do we really need, an expert has answered that it is actually lot less than what we have been taught. On the other hand, though a good night's sleep is vital for good health, overdoing the sleeping can be equally bad for us. But if you sleep less and continue this for too long, the result will be confusion between body and brain signals, resulting in muddled thoughts, lethargic feelings, and overall lassitude. So, the question remains, how many hours of sleep do we really need? Is it essential to sleep the prescribed number of eight hours a day or is catching up a good sleep on a five to six-hour basis enough?

The eight hours of sleep theory is increasingly becoming unpractical in this fast-paced lifestyle. Actually, the recommendation of eight hours of sleep arises based on the idea that our ancestors had their beauty sleep between 8-9 hours in the past. In today's context, this concept is regarded more or less as a myth. In a study conducted by the Sleep Research Center, youngsters within the age group of 8 to 17 generally sleep for about nine hours during the night. However, in the case of adults, this theory is not applicable as a majority of them are sleepless and many of them thrive after a solid sleep varying between 5-7 hours.

A research conducted by the National Institute of Health has established that people who sleep soundly for nine hours a day or more are actually two times more vulnerable than those who sleep less in developing Parkinson's disease. A study report released by the Diabetes Care states that people claiming to sleep less than five hours or more than nine hours daily are the ones with the highest risk of attracting diabetes. In contrast, a large number of contemporary studies prove that people with sleeping patterns that do not exceed or fall beyond seven hours daily possess the highest survival rate. The persons who experience sleeping disorders and sleep less than 4.5 hours have the worst survival rate.

When ascertaining the correct number of hours you should sleep, the fact is that there is no magic number of hours. It will depend on a person to person basis as well as factors like age, activity, and performance level. For example, smaller children and teenagers require more sleep compared to adults. Your personal requirements will not be the same as your friend or colleague who is of the same age and gender as you. Because your sleep needs are unique and individual. According to the National Sleep Foundation, the difference of sleep requirements between two people of the same age, gender, and activity level is due to their basal sleep needs and sleep debt.

Your basal sleep need is the number of hours of sleep you typically need to engage in optimal performance levels. The sleep debt comprises of the accumulated number of hours of sleep you have lost as a result of poor sleeping habits, a recent sickness, social demands, environmental factors, etc. A healthy adult generally possesses a basal sleep need between seven and eight hours each night. If you have experienced sleeping difficulties and as a result accumulated a sleep debt you will find that your performance level is not up to its usual standard, even if you wake up after seven or eight hours of restful sleep. The symptoms will be most apparent during the times the circadian rhythm naturally alters like during mid-afternoon or overnight. One of the ways of easing out of an accumulated sleep debt situation is to get a few extra hours of sleep for a couple of nights until you regain your natural sleeping rhythm and vitality during the day.

Understand what Kind of a Sleeper Are You?

Sleep, dear reader, is the precious restorative that rights so many physical and mental wrongs. The elixir that transforms life and puts a spring in your step, a smile on your face, and the feeling that you can take care of everything that comes your way is sleep. Undervalued, ignored, and forgotten until you wake up to the realization that it's one of the essential foundations of daily wellbeing.

So what kind of a sleeper are you? There are many studies and descriptions of how we sleep but the common consensus settles for the following five simple categories:

1. Lively, healthy early risers!

These happy individuals usually get the sleep they need and rarely feel exhausted or fatigued. They are typically younger than the other groups, usually married or with a long-term partner, working full-time and definitely a morning person with no serious medical conditions.

2. Relaxed and retired seniors.

This is the oldest group in the survey with half of the sample being 65 or older. They sleep the most with an average of 7.3 hours per night compared to 6.8 across all groups. Sleep disorders are rare even though there is a significant proportion with at least one medical disorder.

3. Dozing drones.

These busy people are usually married/partnered and employed but they often work much longer than forty hours a week. Frequently working up to the hour when they go to bed, they get up early so they're always short of sleep and struggle to keep up with the daily pressures of life. Statistically, they'll feel tired or fatigued at least three days a week.

4. Galley slaves.

This group works the longest hours and often suffers from weight problems as well as an unhealthy reliance on caffeine to get through the day. Shift workers often fall into this group and there is also a marked tendency to be a night owl or evening person. They get the least amount of sleep and are more likely to take naps yet, surprisingly, this group often believes that, despite the state of their health, they are getting enough sleep.

5. Insomniacs.

Here is the largest proportion of night people and many of them quite rightly believe they have a sleep problem. About half of this group feel they get less sleep than they need and the same proportion admits to feeling tired, fatigued and lacking energy most of the time.

So, which of the five groups do you think you fit into?

If you're a happy member of Group One, your sleep should by definition be absolutely fine. Don't worry. We've got some really good ideas to share with you to keep you right on track and we'll even add some special extra features to your nightly rest routine to maximize the experience. If you're not in this group, our aim is to help you become a full-time member of the healthy, happy sleepers' association! Membership is for life.

Group Three represents too many tired, irritable, and generally inefficient individuals whose quality of life is impaired because they're too tired too often. Their work suffers because they rarely have sufficient rest to successfully assimilate the day's events. Their home life is degraded because work intrudes too often and they're just too tired to enjoy the pleasures and comfort of a life away from work. Feeling tired becomes their default position and they know they need to do something to give their minds and bodies the rest they deserve. Individuals in this group frequently suffer from long- term mental, physical and emotional stress.

The fourth group is rightly described as the night owls. They work the longest hours and, as we noted above, they typically work shifts. The health problems associated with this group include a marked tendency towards obesity as well as a range of inflammatory diseases. Despite the fact that these people rarely look or feel well, they seem to ignore the evidence and usually claim to get enough sleep, relying on sugary energy drinks and caffeine to keep them awake during waking hours. They take naps because their bodies can't function without additional sleep during the day. An objective analysis of their health would typically reveal a range of health and wellbeing issues.

Insomniacs are the dominant members of Group Five, people who don't get enough sleep, can't get to sleep, and who know they have a problem. Unfortunately, many insomniacs end up taking prescription medication to deal with their symptoms and we have to question the benefits of this solution in light of the many unpleasant side effects associated with long-term sleeping pill dependency. For insomniacs, life is a constant struggle because of the accumulative effects of long-term sleep deprivation.

Health issues abound, depression becomes a major risk, their ability to function normally is often impaired, and they lose sight of their potential to deal successfully with life's daily challenges. They sometimes refer to their condition as living in a nightmare world where they are constantly exhausted and simply cannot function. It's completely understandable that a doctor would prescribe sleeping drugs because the dangers of sleep deprivation can be acute.

Before we begin to examine the practicalities of sleep, we need to know how much sleep is appropriate for each of us as individuals. It's not surprising that different age groups have different sleep requirements.

For example, very young children and infants can sleep in total for around 14 - 15 hours a day. And if you've got teenagers, you might have guessed that adolescents usually need more sleep than adults. Teens can easily sleep between 8.5 to 9.5 hours a night.

It's widely understood that during the first trimester, pregnant women often find they need a lot more sleep than usual. The fact is that if you feel tired during the day, find yourself yawning or taking a nap, you're short on sleep. And this is the time for you to do something practical, realistic, and effective to take care of the problem.

There are many myths surrounding the condition known as OAS or Obstructive Sleep Apnea. It's estimated that around 18 million Americans suffer from the condition but the numbers could be much higher because many people don't report the condition to their doctors. This condition is far more than just loud snoring, although snoring can be a sign of sleep apnea.

People with this condition skip breathing 400 times during the night. The delay in breathing can last from ten to thirty seconds and is then followed by a loud snore as breathing suddenly resumes. The normal sleep cycle is interrupted and this can leave sufferers feeling tired and exhausted during the day. It is a serious condition, especially since it can lead to accidents at work, problems when driving, as well as increasing the risk of heart attacks and strokes. It can affect people of all ages, including children, but tends to affect people more after the age of forty.

Weight also plays a part and there is evidence that shedding excess pounds can improve the condition. Despite all the advice and overwhelming evidence, there are still surprising numbers of sleep apnea sufferers who continue to smoke. Smoking is a perfect way to increase the severity and risks of this debilitating condition.

If you've already trimmed your weight, quit smoking and tried sleeping on your side but still suffer from the condition, you need to see your doctor. There are many treatments available including a special mask that delivers constant air flow to keep the breathing passage open. Lifestyle choices can clearly make a positive difference, too.

Your body, your brain, your mind and your emotional functioning all rely on sufficient sleep to operate efficiently. If you don't get enough sleep, everything suffers. Research suggests that it's much harder than you might imagine to adapt having less sleep than your body needs. The sleep deficit has to be repaid at some point or we'll experience increasingly severe problems.

Simple techniques of preparing for bed

1. Try to get to bed early. The recharging of the body's adrenal system usually takes place between 11p.m. and 1a.m. in the morning. The gallbladder uses the same time to release the toxin build up in the body. If you happen to be awake when both these functions are taking place within your body, there is the possibility of the toxin backing up to the liver which can endanger your health very badly. Sleeping late are byproducts of modern living styles. However, the human body was created in synchronization of nature and its activities. That is why before the advent of electricity people used to go to bed just after sundown and wake up with sunrise.

2. Don't alter your bedtimes haphazardly. Try to stick to a pattern where you go to bed and wake up at the same time. This should be done even on weekends. The continuous pattern will help your body to fit into a rhythm.

3. Maintain a soothing bedtime routine. This can change from person to person. You can use deep breathing exercises, meditation, use of aromatherapy, a gentle relaxing massage given by your partner, or even going through a complete and relaxing skin care routine. The secret is to get into a rhythm which makes you comfortable, relaxed, and ready for bed. Repeating it every day will help in easing out the tensions of the day.

4. Refrain from taking any heavy fluids two hours before bed time. This habit will minimize the number of times you need to visit the bathroom in the middle of the night. You should also make a habit of going to the bathroom just before you get into bed, so that you will not get the urge during night time.

5. Eat a meal enriched with proteins several hours before your bed time. The protein will enhance the production of L-tryptophan which is essential for the production of serotonin and melatonin. Follow up your meal with some fruit to help the tryptophan to cross easily across the blood brain barrier.

6. Refrain from taking any snacks while in bed or just before bed and reduce the level of sugar and grains in your dinner time as it will raise the blood sugar level, delaying sleep. When the body starts metabolizing these elements and the blood sugar level start dropping you will find yourself suddenly awake and unable to go back to sleep.

7. A hot bath before bed is found to be very soothing. When the body temperature is stimulated to a raised level during late evening by the time you get into bed, it will be ready to drop, signaling slumber time to your brain.

8. Stop your work and put them away ideally one to two hours before bed. The interval between work and bedtime should be used for unwinding from the pressure and tension of work. It is essential that you approach your bed with a calm mind instead of being hyped up about some matter.

9. If you prefer reading, a novel with an uplifting story instead of a stimulating one like suspense or mystery is recommended. Or the

suspense will keep you up half the night awake trying to visualize the end to the mystery!

A Few Lifestyle Suggestions to Make You Sleep Better

Don't take medications and drugs unless it is absolutely necessary for your health and wellbeing. A majority of prescribed and over the counter drugs can cause changes in your sleeping patterns.

Avoid drinks with alcohol or caffeine. Caffeine takes longer to metabolize in the body so that your body will experience its effects much longer after consumption. That is why even the cup of coffee you had in the evening will keep you awake during the night. Some of the medications and drugs in the market also contain caffeine which account for their capacity to generate sleeping irregularities. Though alcohol can make you feel drowsy the effect is very much short lived. Once the feeling goes away, you will find that sleep is eluding you for many hours and even the sleep that you finally reach will not take you to deep slumber after alcohol. In the absence of deep sleep, your body will not be able to perform its usual healing and regeneration process is vital for lasting healthiness.

Engage in regular exercise activities. If you are contained in an 8-hour office job, you should make sure that your body receives plenty of exercise which can dramatically increase your sleep health. The best time to exercise is, however, not closer to your bedtime but in the morning.

Keep away from sensitive food types that will keep you awake at night like sugar, pasteurized dairy foods, and grains. These foods can result in congestion, leading to gastric disorders.

The sleep apnea risk is enhanced amongst people with weight issues. If you think you have gained a few extra pounds and during this time you have also experienced sleeping trouble focus on losing the extra weight as a priority. The sleeping issue will correct automatically.

If your body is going through a hormone upheaval like during menopausal or premenopausal time, seek advice from your family physician, as this time can lead to sleeping difficulties.

Want to read more? Purchase our book on **Effective Guide On How to Sleep Well Everyday** *today!*

References

https://www.urbandictionary.com/define.php?term=Trust%20issues

https://thriveworks.com/blog/trust-issues/

https://www.2knowmyself.com/How_to_tell_if_someone_has_trust_issues

https://www.psychalive.org/trust-issues/

https://www.radicalhappiness.com/blog/319-how-childhood-experiences-damage-trust

https://www.goodtherapy.org/blog/the-psychology-of-trust-issues-and-ways-to-overcome-them

https://exploringyourmind.com/pistanthrophobia-afraid-to-trust-others/

https://www.psychologytoday.com/ca/blog/the-athletes-way/201508/the-neuroscience-trust

https://www.bizjournals.com/bizjournals/how-to/human-resources/2014/11/what-to-do-when-you-dont-trust-someone.html

https://medium.com/@swati_jena/you-are-hiding-something-4-reasons-we-find-it-difficult-to-trust-those-we-love-22418f46dac3

https://www.bustle.com/p/9-small-habits-that-can-diminish-trust-in-your-relationship-15732942

https://www.kbrs.ca/insights/could-lack-employee-engagement-be-hurting-your-bottom-line

https://www.bustle.com/p/7-signs-you-havent-dealt-with-past-trust-issues-its-affecting-your-relationship-9017607

https://www.refinery29.com/en-us/trust-issues-new-relationship

https://www.mindbodygreen.com/0-22729/21-signs-you-dont-trust-yourself.html

https://thriveworks.com/blog/trust-issues/

https://blog.mindvalley.com/how-to-trust-again/

http://www.wasatchfamilytherapy.com/archives/4035

https://www.entitymag.com/dealing-with-trust-issues/

https://www.meetmindful.com/how-can-i-overcome-trust-issues/#

https://theunboundedspirit.com/self-doubt/

https://www.capitolstandard.com/this-is-how-you-grow-some-balls-and-start-trusting-yourself/

https://www.healthline.com/health/trusting-yourself#building-trust

https://www.psychologytoday.com/ca/blog/compassion-matters/201506/5-ways-build-trust-and-honesty-in-your-relationship

Printed in Great Britain
by Amazon